W9-BZL-848

GETTING THEM SOBER

VOLUME 2

TOBY RICE DREWS

Bridge Publishing, Inc.
South Plainfield, New Jersey 07080

Also by Toby Rice Drews available from
Bridge Publishing, Inc.:

Getting Them Sober, Volume 1
Getting Them Sober, Volume 3
Getting Rid of Anxiety and Stress

Getting Them Sober, Volume Two
Copyright © 1983 by Toby Rice Drews
All rights reserved
Printed in the United States of America
Library of Congress Catalog Card Number: 80-82751
International Standard Book Number: 0-88270-560-1
Bridge Publishing, Inc., South Plainfield, NJ 07080

Contents

1 Your Children 1

2 Adult Children of Alcoholics 10

3 What if You Are Separated and Your
   Alcoholic Says He'll Get Help? 22

4 What to Expect From
   Your Spouse's Sobriety 31

5 His "Good Stuff" Is as Hooking
   as His "Bad Stuff" 38

6 Carrying Excited Misery
   Into Your Next Relationship 48

7 Being Good to Yourself
   Is Your Quickest and Best Therapy 58

8 How Do I Know if He's Sincere *This*
   Time About Staying Sober? 67

9 If It's Good for You, It's Good for Him 78

10 Verb-Love Versus Noun-Love 84

11 Nothing Makes You Feel Crazier
   Than Sexual Games 89

12 If Your Alcoholic Spouse—or Someone
   Else—Says That *You* Have a
   Drinking and/or Pill Problem 98

13   Could You Be Hiding Behind
      Your Religion? 107

14   Intervention: Forcing the Alcoholic
      to Get Sober 112

15   Trust Your Gut Feeling
      in Working with Professionals 119

16   The Alcoholic and the Kids
      vs. "Mean Mommy" 128

17   Praying for People You
      Justifiably Resent 135

18   Dealing with Irrational Guilt 139

19   Saying Alcoholism Is a Disease Goes
      Deeper Than We Think 143

20   You're Not Trapped 147

21   From Rage to Pity: a Trap 153

22   Getting Help................................... 162

23   If You and the Alcoholic Are Separated
      and You Cannot Stop Being
      Afraid or Angry 168

24   Will Counseling Help a
      Drinking Alcoholic? 175

25   Vacillation Is Okay: You're Not Crazy 182

26   If You're Remarried to Your Second
      Alcoholic, or You've Remarried the Same
      One or You're Dating a Man with a
      Drinking Problem........................... 188

A Fable

(For those persons who feel that they can deal with the disease of alcoholism *all by themselves*.)

There was once a clergyman who lived in a town that was hit by a major flood. The water was a foot deep in his living room. Some parishioners in a boat rowed up to his door, asking him to join them. "No, go ahead," the clergyman replied. "I'll be just fine. God is taking care of me." So they left.

Then the water rose to the second floor. Back came his anxious parishioners in the boat. Again they asked him to join them. Again he refused.

By the time the boat came back once more, the house had been completely engulfed and the clergyman was standing on his chimney. "Reverend," his parishioners called to him, "Come with us! You'll drown."

"No," the clergyman replied. "I'll be fine. The Lord is providing."

So they left. And he drowned.

Later, in heaven, the clergyman angrily made an appointment to see God. "Why did you do this to me?" the clergyman fumed. "I did what you said. I prayed. And you didn't help me."

"Didn't help you?" God answered in surprise. "What do you mean? I sent a boat around to get you three times."

Foreword

The response to the first volume of *Getting Them Sober* has been awesome: I've received many hundreds of letters and phone calls from throughout the U.S. and around the world, from people who read and reread the book, who underline it, read it before they go to sleep, and when they awaken; and who, themselves, gave dozens of copies to their families, in-laws, and to puzzled professionals and to other despairing families of alcoholics.

This past year I have used the first volume of *Getting Them Sober* as a counseling tool in my own treatment groups. I had the groups reread each chapter during the beginning of each session; then, having culled questions from each chapter, I handed out work sheets to the group members and had them write their ideas in response to the questions. After discussion, I would suggest activities for the week to come and I would let the group members share the results during the next session.

Out of that process grew the idea for the Study/Action Guide that you will find at the end of each chapter in this volume. Individual family members will find it to be a gentle helping hand to lead them into solutions for their troubles; groups and classrooms will be able to use it as a built-in counseling/teaching aid.

Together, volumes one and two of *Getting Them Sober,* and *Getting Them Sober (Action Guide)*, are meant to help provide a solid healing base from which real strides can be made by the family, in their ongoing treatment, in Al-Anon and counseling.

The purpose of Volume 2 is to further help eradicate those secret fears and to expose more alcoholic patterns to the light, so families feel less isolated and begin to realize they can get well.

I would like to thank all the people who so considerately contacted me over the past two years, and gave me feedback and encouragement. They shared their problems and their successes with me. When they hurt, I hurt, and when they grew, I grew.

—Toby Rice Drews

Acknowledgments

Many special thanks to:

Margaret Hartnett, of *The Journal of Nursing Administration,* for her suggestions and encouragement; Dr. James R. Milam, author of *Under the Influence* (a book I highly recommend to families in order to deepen their understanding of the depth of the disease of alcoholism), for his ongoing encouragement; and Lloyd Hildebrand, my editor, for his flexibility, caring, and support.

1

Your Children

Alcoholism is a family disease.
You can help your children.
You are not responsible for another person's behavior.

The families of alcoholics are forced to cope with their loved one's "craziness." This directly affects each family member in individual ways. The spouse and the children become the innocent victims of the disease. It is important to realize that there is support available—both for spouses and for children.

It is really important for the spouse of an alcoholic, who is usually the one person in the family who goes for help, to seek an Al-Anon group because of the healing she will find there. It's also a good idea for such a woman to compel her children to get help in Al-Ateen, if they're between eleven and nineteen years of age. It is advisable for younger children to go to a pre-teen group, for five- to eleven-year-olds.

Al-Ateen will help your youngsters to understand

1

themselves and the factors that influence their behavior. They will learn how they have had to adjust to their family sickness, and the general causes and effects of alcoholism. As they grow in their understanding of the sickness and its impact on family relationships and behavior, they will be enabled to cope with their guilt feelings and to grow in self-worth.

Often, I hear mothers say, "My children don't want to get help." If your child had chicken pox you'd take him to a doctor, no matter how he felt. Since you, as the non-alcoholic spouse, have learned to deny so much, understandably, from living with an alcoholic for all those years, you have a pattern that's hard to break. Denial combined with guilt makes us very prone to say of certain situations that they are not really serious.

By the term "denial" I mean that the spouse of an alcoholic tries, out of her terror, to pretend that there is no problem—to deny the existence of alcoholism in the mate. This results in a whole chain of problems.

I think that many times spouses of alcoholics feel very guilty that their children could have been made sick from the disease of alcoholism. They have this guilt even though they may know, *intellectually,* that they don't control or cause—especially don't *cause*—this disease. They beat themselves to death by saying, "Oh, I should have left him long ago," or "I should have stopped him from doing this or that."

2

If this is how you feel, *you have to learn not to forgive yourself. To forgive yourself is to say that you did something wrong; but you didn't. You're up against a disease.*

I know it doesn't seem like that. It seems like you got a rotten man, a weird man, a strange person, an alcoholic who is violent and abusive and irresponsible. In spite of all this you feel like somehow you should be able to handle all the rotten situations in that household. But you're simply not responsible for those problems, even though you may strongly feel that way.

None of us who are closely involved with an alcoholic are responsible for his disease. What we are responsible for, however, is *our* recovery from it. We must begin with "baby steps." And once you've been to Al-Anon for a while it's good to start looking at your children, attempting to identify behavior patterns that could later become very destructive to them.

Statistics indicate that two-thirds of children with one alcoholic parent marry alcoholics and/or become alcoholics themselves. If they have two alcoholic parents there's close to a hundred percent chance of these outcomes taking place. So getting these kids to treatment is very important.

Your youngest child could be one who clowns around, and is very bright and witty. He performs a lot and keeps the family laughing, etc. You may, therefore, think, "Well, he doesn't have a problem."

But this is so typical of the behavior of the youngest children of alcoholics. The oldest child frequently becomes an adult too early, a kind of overly responsible surrogate parent. The middle child gets kind of lost. These patterns are not hard and fast, but they reappear very frequently. To make a virtue out of these behavior patterns in your children is to unconsciously deny that there's anything wrong.

These observations are not designed to make you feel that you're bad or that you went wrong somewhere. Try to look at it like this. If all of a sudden a plague came through your area that nobody ever heard of before and your children caught it, you wouldn't feel responsible, would you? The disease of alcoholism, and its effects, are very much like this.

Try to look at alcoholism as a disease; that's exactly what it is. You cannot be held responsible for what happened to those kids. I'm sure you did your best. I've never seen the spouse of an alcoholic who didn't try so very, very hard to be the perfect mother and who didn't beat herself to death about having made the kinds of mistakes that *all* human beings are capable of making. In fact, I think your efforts are probably rather heroic, considering what you have to contend with. The efforts of the non-alcoholic spouse to be a good parent are usually, to say the least, very heroic.

What happens when children grow up without being treated for their "inherited" disease? They often become rescuers; they usually become deniers.

They frequently go into the helping professions, bringing their denial and guilt with them. If they've been to Al-Ateen, however, they learn to drop a lot of that kind of behavior. They learn to feel that they don't have to rescue the world, that they don't have to always overachieve.

Very often, when grown children of alcoholics think of marriage, they either unconsciously find an alcoholic or they deliberately look for someone who is not an alcoholic, but who turns out to be another child of an alcoholic who either does not drink at all or does so only moderately. But unfortunately what I've seen too many times is that these two grown children of alcoholics, because they're carrying the typical alcoholic family "baggage" with them, act out the behavior patterns of an alcoholic marriage, minus the alcohol. Then what happens? Frequently, *their* children, since they grow up in a household where the behavior patterns are basically those of an alcoholic and a non-alcoholic spouse of an alcoholic, also develop alcoholic behavior patterns. It becomes a pattern that repeats itself, generation after generation—until the affected individuals identify the problem areas and take steps to break the cycle. Al-Anon and Al-Ateen show them how.

As you can see, alcoholism is a very insidious disease. I have counseled hundreds of wives of alcoholics who are not aware of the behavior patterns they have learned and taken into their marriages. They also don't realize that unless their children get treatment they too will be in danger of becoming alcoholics. For these reasons, Al-Anon and Al-Ateen are essential.

If you experience difficulty in getting your children to agree to go to Al-Ateen, you may want to say something like, "Look, you only have to go to eight meetings. After that, it's up to you." You can usually make a younger child go to a pre-teen group, but for the teenager in your household, it is a good idea to encourage him to just "try it out" and see whether he likes it.

If a particular Al-Ateen group does not suit your teenagers, then encourage them to go to other such groups until they find the one in which they can feel comfortable. If they still adamantly refuse to go to Al-Ateen, and they're in their middle or late teens and you really don't feel that you can convince them that they should go, it is best for you to simply drop the subject for a while. As *you* go to Al-Anon and/or treatment for yourself and *you* become a calmer person, and *you* feel better and become an example to your children, then often, when the children begin dating or they encounter engagement or marital problems themselves, they'll often turn to you and indicate a willingness to go to Al-Anon meetings with you. Everybody wins then; it just takes time.

"Permit the little children to come unto me, and forbid them not: for of such is the kingdom of God." (Mark 10:14)

Facts:

1. All family members neurotically "adjust" to the alcoholic's addiction pattern. Without treatment, they keep this problem throughout their lives. It "sets in" and gets worse.

2. The most characteristic symptom of all is the broadening of the alcoholic's denial syndrome to the entire family.

Write About:

1. "My oldest child is my comfort and my confidante—and does not need treatment."

2. "My youngest is so outgoing and clever; how can he or she possibly need help?"

3. Don't tell me my well-behaved, quiet child will grow up to marry and/or become an alcoholic."

4. "My kids refuse to go to treatment."

Suggested Activities:

1. Each time you start to berate yourself for "subjecting your kids to the alcoholic," tell yourself that *that's* your disease talking. The disease keeps you sick by keeping you guilty and, therefore, you are less able to make positive changes. How are you supposed to cure or control a disease when no one else can?

2. Start to approach one of your children about the idea of going to Al-Ateen or pre-teen groups. These are for children of alcoholics, aged five to nineteen.

2

Adult Children of Alcoholics

One hour a week in Al-Anon can take away ten hours a week of emotional pain.

"Alcoholic denial" isn't just denial about drinking; it's pretending you weren't pathologically affected by the disease.

Survivors get help.

I am the child of an alcoholic and I know how you feel. After you get out of an alcoholic family situation you may say, "I feel like a bird let out of a cage. I got away from all of that junk; I never want to hear about alcoholism again, I'm tired of it. I'm never going to do what my mother did; I'm *never* going to marry an alcoholic!" You either give this message to yourself overtly, or you unconsciously believe that you will never marry nor become an alcoholic. You've had it—that's all there is to it.

Very well. But do you find yourself attracted to needy people, to needy members of the opposite sex?

Do you find yourself dating very neurotic men, or guys who are just drinking too much? Do you find yourself hanging around bars to meet guys even if you yourself are not drinking, drinking very little, or just drinking Perrier water? Do you find yourself attracted to exciting guys who are not very nice? Do you find yourself bored with guys who are very good to you? If you're wincing at this description, I would say that you're one of the many children of alcoholics who's well on her way to marrying an alcoholic.

I don't think it's necessary to spend ten years in therapy to find out why you're going along with this kind of stuff. I think that knowing *why* is not important; I don't even know if you can find out why you're doing these things. It's analogous to the still-drinking alcoholic who has been going to a psychiatrist for twenty years, trying to find out the root causes of his alcoholism in the hopes that eventually he will be able to stop drinking.

Too many alcoholics have died that way. Sure, they find out the root causes of all kinds of things. But what they don't realize is that you first have to get the booze out of the body before the mind will clear. *You stop drinking first.*

And I think it's just as important for the adult children of alcoholics to realize the route they're taking—to say, "I don't have to spend twenty years in therapy and twenty thousand dollars to try to figure out why I'm acting like this."

I think it's really quite simple. You learned these

behavior patterns unconsciously from your alcoholic family and you're acting out the responses you learned. The only thing left to do is to stop acting them out. And one doesn't learn to stop acting out behavior patterns by just deciding not to act them out. You need a *healing* process—a behavioral healing process—and you will get that in Al-Anon and Al-Ateen.

I've talked to many grown women who are daughters of alcoholics. They often don't want to go to Al-Anon. They say, "Oh, it's for those wives of alcoholics. I'm not married to one and I don't want to marry one. What would I do there?" What you might want to do is to go to Al-Anon for a while and find some people who want to join together and form a special kind of Al-Anon group for adult children of alcoholics. Meanwhile, getting yourself to Al-Anon will help you to start breaking those behavior patterns you learned earlier. They really amount to a lack of self-esteem. You are unconsciously drawn towards somebody who will stay with you because you prove to him how good you will be for him. Basically, he may seem strong, but the opposite is really the case. *He* is needy, not you, *but you wind up feeling as if* you *are the needy one.* Really, you will become the "caretaker," one way or the other. The emotional and/or financial responsibilties—among others—will become yours.

You know, there's a pride thing involved in this too, an understandable human pride. You think,

"No. Who needs Al-Anon? Not me!"

Well, unfortunately, that's just the way the alcoholic talks. Remember how your alcoholic parent would get you so frustrated by saying, "I can do it myself"? Are you perhaps imitating that kind of behavior? We *learn* that kind of improper use of self-sufficiency. If you look at alcoholism truly as a disease—which is exactly what it is—then it makes perfect sense to *treat* it as a disease. Try to see Al-Anon as a medicine for your family's disease—that's all it is, pure and simple. An hour-long meeting every week isn't going to take that much time out of a busy schedule. Also it's very effective therapy, and it's free. With families economizing right and left these days, why spend sixty-five dollars or more per hour in therapy when you can get it free in Al-Anon?

If you need counseling in addition to Al-Anon, that's fine. But get the basics in Al-Anon. If you have to go to therapy too, the combination of Al-Anon and therapy will speed up the getting-well process.

What does that mean in practical terms? It will promote faster family healing, enabling you to reach the point where you can start feeling very good about yourself. It means you will not want to be bogged down with crazy relationships and going back and forth into your "excited misery" again. It means you will be able to find and select a boyfriend or a mate who will be very good to you. You will be able to accept the relationship, and love your partner openly instead of going through life all bogged down over the disease of alcoholism. Isn't it worth the investment of an hour a week, regardless of any preconceived ideas you may have about Al-Anon?

You'll find that the meetings can be very healing, very comforting. You'll learn to feel very precious. You'll also learn that you don't have to go the route of being addicted to an attractive, pathological individual, who will say all of the "hooking" words to get you into what will be a precarious relationship at best.

It is very important for you to realize that you don't have to look at this as an all-or-nothing picture (which is a typical response that is part and parcel of the disease). You don't have to say, "Oh, this is so depressing. I'm going to have to go to Al-Anon for the rest of my life." Instead of worrying about the future, why don't you just go for *now* and see how you like it after a couple of months. Go once a week or however often you want for a few weeks; look around for a sponsor, someone who has a pretty together, comfortable, happy life right now, who has taken the route you're afraid you might be on, whom you'd feel comfortable calling, if necessary, between meetings. Get that person's phone number.

The point is also that if you get the help now and you learn to change those unconscious behavior patterns in a relatively short period of time, you can help break that family pattern of alcoholism and not have it go on for generations. Then you can marry somebody who's *good* to you and raise *healthy*

14

children instead of children who themselves have a 65 percent chance of marrying an alcoholic and/or becoming an alcoholic themselves.

Often, it's that "self-image junk" that stops us from getting well. I am referring to the approach that "I am a strong person; I don't need to get help. I can lick this myself. And if I can't lick this particular thing myself I'm a failure and I don't want people to know it." That's an understandable attitude. But, if we contract a disease, *then the only way we can fail is to fail to treat it.* It is really a sign of strength to accept the fact that we have to get help. It's a sign of coping; it's a sign of survival. To realistically know one's limitations is a sign of a well-adjusted person who can assess a situation and say, "Okay, I tried to beat it myself for a while, and it seems I'm getting more and more mired into this alcoholism junk for some reason. So I'm going to try the route of getting some help for a while and see what happens."

After all, putting your head in the sand and pretending everything's okay isn't going to make it work. In fact, that is a reflection of the basic symptom of the whole disease—*denial.* Denial will do nothing but put you right on the road, willing or not, towards alcoholism.

It's totally understandable. I completely empathize and sympathize with your wanting to just forget all about alcoholism; you've had it up to here. Well, going to Al-Anon doesn't mean that you have to think about alcoholism twenty-four hours a day, no

15

Facts:

1. All people have "blind spots" (their denials) about their behavior patterns. That's one of the reasons why many therapists themselves are required, by their professions, to go through therapy for themselves.

2. Most people anticipate more pain than comfort in a therapeutic situation. They may see Al-Anon and Al-Ateen in this same light. They don't realize, at first, that it is possible, in a group counseling session, to take what you want and leave the rest. They may not understand that if one encounters something that is too painful to deal with, one can "put it on the shelf"—to perhaps think about another time. They often don't realize that going for help can be a matter of just going for comfort, and that this is a legitimate approach to treatment. It involves being gentle with yourself.

Write About:

1. "I don't want to hear/see/think about alcoholism again!"

2. "I'm *not* going to wind up like my mother and marry an alcoholic, and I don't need Al-Anon to help me with that."

3. "I'm not going to Al-Anon because I don't identify with them."

4. "I get emotional 'twinges' when I think about my overall dating/marriage patterns."

5. "I tend always to be trying to do the most and create the best. It's never really enough."

6. "I tend to travel around with friends from other 'flawed' families."

7. "Way down deep I'd like to be accepted by the 'self-assured majority' that have never known alcoholism in their families."

8. "I don't know any 'normal' families. If I do, and I go around with them, I seem to attract all the 'strange people,' even though there are very few of them around these well-adjusted people. If they're there, they'll be attracted to me. I don't know why this happens."

9. "I don't want to go for treatment because *I'm* a survivor and I don't want to seem, even to myself, that I've been affected by alcoholism!"

Suggested Activities:

1. Tell yourself that it takes strength, not weakness, to acknowledge a problem and not pretend, like a child would, that all your problems will just go away.

2. Let yourself be free to explore six Al-Anon meetings before deciding whether or not to continue going.

3. Instead of seeing treatment as a burden, allow it to help unburden you from the pain of rotten relationships, past, present and future.

3

What if You Are Separated and Your Alcoholic Says He'll Get Help?

If it's good for you, it's good for him.

If it's good for you, it's going to be good for your children.

Your guilt (when you do what makes you feel good) is your disease talking.

If the alcoholic gets angry when you do what makes you more peaceful, that's his disease talking.

What I'm going to say here is not a hard-and-fast rule. I know you are trying to do the best you can. Sometimes during a time of separation from your spouse, the emotional and financial strain can become too much.

You may find that your alcoholic spouse says he'll get help, and he may promise to go to a psychiatrist. Well, *unless* that psychiatrist is very knowledgable about alcoholism and is AA-oriented, and insists that his clients, who are alcoholics, attend AA on a daily basis during early sobriety, then I would say that that therapist is probably not a good referral for your spouse.

Sometimes an alcoholic does not have a sincere desire to stop drinking even though he says he will get treatment. If he goes to the right psychologist or psychiatrist or social worker, that person may actually increase the alcoholic's pain and awareness of the disease in an effort to get him to want sobriety. Then the counselor will insist that his client go to AA for recovery.

It may be a good idea to stay separated from your alcoholic *if you can* during the first year of sobriety. I know a woman who, when her husband said he was going to get sober, told him, "Look, I know your first year is going to be terrible and I'm not going to deal with that; that's *your* problem." She then proceeded to take her kids and herself back to Missouri. They corresponded and called each other frequently, and when he got settled down after his first year of sobriety, she came back with the kids and they have been living together happily ever since.

It takes a pretty intact woman to be able to do that kind of thing without fear that she will lose her husband in the process. And that's the crux of the matter. Most people who go back to their alcoholics too soon are usually going back because they're afraid their alcoholics will leave them, especially if they've been the kind that say or imply that once they get sober they'll leave. After many years of hearing from him that when he's sober he's a movie star, you almost tend to believe it instead of realizing that when he's sober he's just a regular person.

If you're already separated, a good rule of thumb is to hold out as long as you can financially and/or emotionally until he shows you that he's sincere in his not wanting to drink and in his endeavors to be sober. There's a big difference between not wanting to drink and efforts to be sober. You can want not to drink but if you don't do anything about it, there's a good chance you're going to drink again.

I hear women who say to me over and over again, "My husband's going to AA." When I ask them how often their husbands attend, they generally say that it is once or twice a week. Sure, *some* people stay sober that way, but most do not.

The AA recommendation is *ninety meetings in ninety days.* A woman will ask me nervously, "Suppose my husband doesn't know this?" The fact is he *does* know it, if he's been to an AA-oriented treatment center. They will have told him to go to ninety meetings in ninety days when he gets out. Men in AA will tell him the same thing.

That early sobriety time—the first one to three years in AA—is very, very crucial. People have a much greater chance of staying sober without slips if they attend AA on at least a daily basis, for at least a year.

People who are serious about AA, serious about

staying sober, serious about not being miserable any more, go many times more often than that. Some people, if they're hurting badly, attend as many as three or four meetings a day. During early sobriety it's really important that a person learn to rely on AA.

Can the church help? Yes. Can psychiatry help? Yes. But it is good to remember that when doctors, psychiatrists, pastors and priests become ill with the disease of alcoholism, the physicians and clergy committees will send these individuals to an alcoholism treatment center, and then require them to go to AA on a regular basis.

There is no contradiction and no conflict between going to church and going to AA. As a matter of fact, in the AA "Big Book," called *Alcoholics Anonymous,* it is stressed that it is a very good idea for recovering alcoholics to heal any rifts that they've had with their religion (even if they've been only in their hearts).

One reason why it's generally a good idea for wives not to go back right away to the alcoholic who is getting help is that he may prematurely get the idea that everything is just fine. That gives him the additional impression that his few days at AA were sufficient to deal with his problem and that he doesn't have to go back any more.

During that early time of sobriety, the alcoholic's emotions wander all over the place. It is a time of acute withdrawal from alcohol, and during those first few weeks or months of dryness, the alcoholic is going to be having mood swings, perhaps ten times a day. His range of emotions will go from one extreme to the next. The longer you can hold out from going back, therefore, the less you're going to bear the brunt of his mood changes. If you're with the alcoholic, not only is he going to dump on you, but there's also a good chance that he's going to *lean* on you. And if he leans on you, that means he's going to lean on AA *less*.

Some people will say, "Well, are they going to take care of him in AA?" Sure they are. And that brings me to my next point. If he says that he wants you to go to meetings, because he doesn't want to go alone, it's not a bad idea to go along with him, at least a few times, until he gets used to it. You can also go with him when he goes to a new AA group. But after that, if he wants you along, it's a good idea just to go along with him for the ride, but not for the meeting itself. If possible, select places where you can find Al-Anon and AA groups meeting at the same time, in the same building. Then you can go to the Al-Anon room while he goes to the AA room. There's a good reason for this. Often, after a meeting, if you are in the same room together, he will choose to sit with you and talk with you, instead of a fellow group member. If you're sitting with him others will hesitate to intrude. They will not walk up, introduce themselves, talk to him, offer to help, give him their phone numbers and so forth. However, if he's sitting there by himself, other

AA members will introduce themselves to him, and they will soon be in a position to give him the help that he needs. They'll encourage him to call when he needs help, and offer to be his sponsor. In short, there's a much better chance that he'll be able to get closer to other people in AA if you're not with him at those meetings. And if he leans on you, that means that he's not leaning on the help that he can get from AA. And only they can help him to get and stay sober.

Another thing. Sometimes well-meaning, recovering alcoholics—even if they're counselors—might tell the wife not to go back until her alcoholic is dry for several months. She then goes back, he starts drinking again, and she may sometimes feel that they're blaming her. Even if they do actually blame her, she should bear in mind that, although recovering alcoholics understand *alcoholics,* very often they haven't themselves lived in the craziness of an alcoholic home. They are often completely unaware of the kinds of things that you have gone through. They *think* they're thinking, instead, totally in terms of the welfare of the alcoholic. *They often don't realize that if a situation is good for you, it's therefore good for the alcoholic.*

If you feel you have to go back in order to survive emotionally and/or financially, then that's okay. It's a good idea to ask people in Al-Anon what you can do, instead of asking recovering alcoholics what is the best way to proceed. I think you'll get an answer that is more in tune with your whole family's real needs, if you go to the people in Al-Anon first.

If it's good for you, it's going to be good for your children, too. If it's going to calm you down, it's going to calm your children down. In the long run, that is the best thing for the alcoholic, too. If you get calm and the kids get calm, *even if you didn't follow someone else's time table,* then it takes away some of the guilt from the alcoholic and that's going to help him stay sober. That's going to be much more meaningful to you than if you simply stayed out of the picture for a few more days or weeks. It's more important that you take care of yourself and get well.

And if you have to leave again and come back again, that's okay too.

The tremendous load of guilt that the alcoholic carries, and never wants to talk about, is guilt over damaging his family. And the family should go ahead and get repaired by doing whatever it can to reach the goal of healthful living. Consequently, the family is helping the alcoholic because individual family members are getting well themselves, *whatever* that entails, and that lifts the alcoholic's load of guilt.

The pain of the alcoholic's disease will increase if he continues to drink. That's good because, if the pain gets bad enough, it could motivate him to stop drinking. But it is important to realize that increased guilt doesn't necessarily have the same effect. Taking away some of the guilt and increasing some of the pain from the drinking is often a potent combination to help him want to get the power to stop drinking. You can help take away his guilt by getting well yourself and helping your kids to get well.

That means it is important for *you* to get calm. And it's okay for you to use *any* means you think may be necessary to get calm, even if this involves vacillating back and forth. Put your own feelings of guilt aside. Keep trying to do everything you can to make yourself well, even if it is only in a seemingly raggedy fashion. It's okay; we all try imperfect ways to find peace.

Through your attempts to achieve peace, you will experience less anxiety.[1] One way to reach this goal is to attend meetings of Al-Anon and to take your kids to Al-Ateen. This will produce calmness in your life, and make your kids calm in the long run.

That will help him get sober too.

"God is love." (1 John 4:8)

---

[1] See another book I've written that may help you—*Get Rid of Anxiety and Stress* (Bridge Publishing, South Plainfield, NJ 07080, 1982).

Write On:

1. (Finish this sentence): "I feel so scared that he won't get/stay sober that I want to arrange the whole scene. That includes _____

_____

_____

_____

_____

_____

_____

_____

_____."

Suggested Activity:

1. Each time you try to make everything right so that he'll stay sober, think it through. One person cannot always watch another person to "make sure" they do or don't do something. Besides, alcoholics are going to do what they want, no matter what anyone else says or does.

4

What to Expect From
Your Spouse's Sobriety

The road to recovery is a bumpy one.
*This is a time when it's especially important for
you to do fun things for yourself, daily.*

The matter of confused expectations causes
potential problems in *any* relationship. In a marriage,
such confusion is magnified when one partner's
expectations of certain responses from the other do
not materialize. It is not difficult, therefore, to
understand how these problems are worse in the
home of an alcoholic.

Since everything is sort of backward in an alcoholic
home, anyway, I don't think it's surprising that very
often one has expectations where it's not realistic,
and where one should have expectations, one often
does not.

For example, I spoke to a woman named Helen
whose husband was in his first year of sobriety. She
liked the fact that he was regularly going to AA, that

he had stopped swearing at her, and that he was generally rather pleasant to be around. She said that he was very quiet, but she didn't mind that so much. One thing she *did* mind was that he was always going to meetings and that it seemed they never did anything else as a couple. What she especially did not like was that they didn't go out to dinner the way they used to. (He said that he was afraid to go to restaurants and he didn't know why.)

I think her husband is typical of a lot of alcoholics going through early sobriety. It's so new, it's so scary. And they have toxic fears due to protracted withdrawal that goes on for a year or two. They have to go to daily meetings and sometimes attend two, three or four times a day, even hang out in AA clubhouses between meetings. And of course the wife feels, understandably, very much left out.

I know it's not pleasant for the non-alcoholic spouse to deal with this kind of thing. It often feels as if they're between a rock and a hard place. They want some social life, but fear if he skips meetings in favor of going out socially that he'll start drinking again.

Most alcoholics, however, after the first year or so of sobriety, can start to spend at least one or two evenings with their families every week in a sober, low-key way. Some alcoholics, who were never in really bad shape, can start doing that after the first ninety days. Others may have to wait anywhere from six months to two or three years.

Most alcoholics feel that they do have to go to meetings daily during the first year. After that, many can start to spend a few nights a week with their families. Many alcoholics resolve this problem by going to luncheon or early morning meetings or 5:30 P.M. meetings when they can, thereby getting in their meetings and saving some of their evenings for their families.

Oftentimes, the family, understandably, doesn't realize the damage that alcohol has done to the alcoholic's brain. Each family member needs to realize that successful withdrawal from alcohol dependence is a long process. Many alcoholics in the AA program today are addicted both to alcohol and to other drugs. That makes their withdrawal more difficult and much more emotionally painful. This protracted withdrawal can go on for about eighteen to thirty-six months.

Many alcoholics find that it takes anywhere from six to thirty months to get over their withdrawal. Their symptoms may range from pretty bad depression to very bad compulsion to drink, to tremendous anxiety, paranoia, agitation, inability to sit still, lack of concentration, restlessness, nightmares, muscle spasms, sleeplessness and uncontrollable, seemingly uncaused feelings of rage.

It is too much to expect an alcoholic who is in the midst of all these terrible withdrawal symptoms to sit through a dinner or a play or a concert. When he says he can't do it, he really means it. The repair has to go on; the alcoholic has to go through it. He will come out stronger on the other side. But to expect him to also endure the stress of sitting through an evening out makes it even harder for him to go through his withdrawal.

What's confusing sometimes is that the alcoholic will go along for a few weeks feeling good when all of a sudden the stress of withdrawal will hit again. What happens is that his withdrawal from the drug (of alcohol) goes through cycles of varying intensity. He can feel bad for a few months during early sobriety, then feel good, then feel bad again, and so on. This varies, of course, with each individual and depends on a variety of factors.

Now what can the spouse do during this time? Obviously, you can't go through the withdrawal for him or with him; the only place where he can find real comfort is from his AA meetings and sponsor, perhaps also from an outside therapist. One way to deal with your loneliness is to develop outside interests. Go to your church group, maybe go shopping for the day with friends.

What your spouse is going through is teaching him how to be *independent* and yet *dependent* on AA and his Higher Power. But it is very painful for him to learn how to do this. The same thing goes on with the spouse of an alcoholic. It is often a time of painful growth—both for the alcoholic and the spouse.

What can you expect of your alcoholic during early sobriety? You have a right to expect that he would not "dump on you." If he's feeling all kinds of bad emotions and then turns it around and is sarcastic and very nasty to you and doesn't talk to you for days at a time, I think you can put your foot down and say that you won't permit that kind of behavior. It's okay for him to talk about how bad he feels, but he should not be allowed to dump on you.

I think that withdrawal from alcohol, in many ways, is like a recovery from any other disease. There's going to be a period of rest and recuperation, perhaps a period during which your alcoholic will not be employable. During such a time, the most he'll be able to manage will be the daily AA meetings and hanging around AA clubhouses. But I think that you can at least expect him to be civil to you. Nasty behavior does not have to be part and parcel of getting well. *Such behavior is not going to help him to stay sober.* As a matter of fact, if you allow him to get by with that kind of behavior, you're just reinforcing his belief that he can get away with anything he wants. And that's not helping him to stay sober. Just the opposite. It's helping him to continue to feel like a tin god.

"Please be patient with me. God is not finished with me yet." (Bill Gothard)

35

Suggested Activities:

1. Remind yourself often that not only do you not have to "walk on eggs" so that he'll stay sober, but you could even break the darn eggs over the alcoholic's head, and he'd still stay sober—*if he wants to.*

2. Remind yourself that you are not your alcoholic's caretaker. Whether you stay with him or not, *he* is responsible for the maintenance of his sobriety.

5

His "Good Stuff"
Is as Hooking as His "Bad Stuff"

It's only an illusion that one needs *those occasional loving words; it is a* want, *not a* need.

The increased self-worth you will feel by doing what's good for you, in the long run, *will make you feel* very *good.*

Mariette's husband had left her, this time, for what many might think was a very trivial reason. He had told her one day when she had the flu that he "couldn't take it any more." At first she didn't know what he was talking about, but then she found out that he just could not take the anxiety of living with anybody who had the slightest ailment, even a cold. He didn't put it quite that way. He just got extremely angry with her when she had the flu, said he wasn't going to put up with it any more and walked out.

This time he stayed away for several weeks. Meanwhile, Mariette's ailment had turned into pneumonia.

In spite of this, she was coping rather well and, once she got past the initial terror of living alone, was actually starting to appreciate the calm and peace of the house.

She had formerly thought that she would not want to be separated from him at all because she would worry about him getting involved with another woman. But once he actually left, that fear went out the window and was replaced with the fear of how she was going to manage living by herself. And she found that when she put one foot in front of the other and did what she was supposed to do when she was supposed to do it, no matter how she felt, she found herself getting through each day rather successfully. It was a great comfort to her to learn that the worst, as far as she could see it, had happened—he had walked out—*and she was still all right.*

She didn't yet fully understand how "crazy" alcohol had caused her husband to become. She had lived with this disease for so long that its craziness had become kind of normal to her. Therefore, it didn't seem like craziness to her any more. It seemed like normality. She thought that she was so adjusted to craziness that she would have a very hard time coming back and getting adjusted to normality. But the longer she was away from the alcoholic, the more she found herself getting used to dealing and acting like a regular person. She found that she was adjusting to the normal, real world rather quickly— much quicker, in fact, than she thought she would.

One day, on her birthday, when she came home from work, she found a large card in the mail—one of those oversized studio cards. She opened it and it was a beautiful romantic card from her husband. He had sent her this card that told her what a wonderful person she was, how very special she was to him, how very important, how much he loved her and how he would adore her forever, etc. Completely ignored was the fact that he had left her for weeks and weeks. Nevertheless the card made her feel very special, very wanted; it also made her feel a little crazy. Shortly after she received the card, he called her and asked if he could come back home.

Mariette had told her husband a few months previously that if he ever left again he would have to go through treatment before he came home; that she wasn't going to put up with his behavior any longer. Her therapist was backing her up in this, knowing full well that her husband was going to have to get treatment or he was going to die from alcoholism. If he wanted strongly enough to keep his marriage together, that might be the motivating factor that Mariette could use—the clout, so to speak, that would get him to go to treatment.

Mariette wanted her husband to come back home. She took the card to her therapist to show her how much he really loved her and what a good person he was; how decent, kind, and loving. After all, he had remembered her birthday with a wonderful card.

Her therapist took one look at the card and

snorted. She looked at Mariette and said, "Don't you see how very manipulative this card is?"

Mariette instantly felt as if her therapist had thrown a bucket of cold water in her face. She felt as if the therapist was telling her that not only was her husband rotten to her a lot of the time, but, in addition, when he appeared to be good to her, he wasn't really being good. He was being manipulative. If *that* were all true, what was left? It seemed as if her therapist was taking the whole reason for the existence of her relationship with her husband away from her.

She finally found the courage to tell her therapist this. She replied, "What I'm trying to do is to get you to look at reality. When we deny reality, we just stay sick; and that means that the people we love stay sick too. At first, when we look at the reality, we may be genuinely horrified. But if we take a hard look at the facts and admit to ourselves what *is* and what *isn't* true, *then* we can start to do something about the situations in which we find ourselves. When we don't admit what reality is, then we can't do anything about it because we are not admitting to ourselves that something is wrong."

Mariette then asked her, "Well, what in the world can I do about this? Why do you think he is being manipulative?"

"Look at this," her therapist replied. "I'm not saying that your husband is consciously being manipulative. He probably believes that he's being loving and everything else. But he's driven by a drug—alcohol. He's driven by his disease, alcoholism. That disease is driving him to do everything possible to protect its own existence and continuance. It will tell your husband to do anything to get you to drop the demand for him to get help and treatment for his alcoholism. His disease wants him to convince you to take him back right now, as is, and pretend nothing is wrong so that he can go on drinking and dying. *That's his disease talking. It is not your husband talking.* If it can't reach you through anger, then it's going to reach you through lovey-dovey words. But it's trying to get you to render yourself ineffective in relationship to that disease. So when you say no to your husband and to what he wants, you are really saying no to his disease. That's the most loving thing you can say to your husband. You have to let him know that he can't wind you around his little finger and get back in that house and continue to drink and act as if everything is just fine, if only he says nice words.

Mariette went to Al-Anon. She learned to lean on her Higher Power and not feel alone, and to get through this very tough period. Her husband got into treatment.

Now I realize that a lot of you are in the same situation right now. It's very scary. You're probably saying to yourself, "I can't say no if he wants to come back, even if he won't get help. I'm too scared." But a lot of times what's underneath all these doubts is the very terrible fear that you'll lose this man.

Let's look at it. What's the worst that can happen? Suppose you lose him. I never heard of anybody dying from losing a person. And remember, if he continues to drink and doesn't get help for his alcoholism, you *will* lose him. Nobody gets past the fact that alcoholism is a progressive, fatal disease. Now if you can't say no to him and to his disease at this time and if you feel like you will just fall apart if he doesn't come home when he wants to, then it's *okay* for now. Put this information on the shelf. Let yourself know that someday, should he do this again, you may have the courage to carry through on this. *God really does help us in our weakness.* Sometimes when we feel that we're at our worst and we can't help and that all we can do is to give in to the situation, God in His mercy will come in and do for us what we cannot do for ourselves.

Try to leave yourself open to God's intervention. Events may take another twist, another route, so that your husband gets treatment. Meanwhile, the most important thing for you to do is to *try to get well*. If you can say no, and it makes him go into treatment, okay. If you can't say no and you have to take your husband back, it's okay. Do whatever you have to do to get through today.

There is another way in which your husband's "nice" ways of treating you can be just as "hooking" as his negative ways of treating you. I had a client

43

named Jane whose husband was very cruel to her. The last time he walked out, she thought she would fall apart. But she didn't. After living with a succession of other women, he started to woo her again by bringing her flowers and gifts. She began to feel that maybe this time it would be different. She would take him back, and back he would come— until he decided to go out again. This kind of thing went on for years, back and forth, back and forth. Jane started to realize, since going to Al-Anon and going to therapy, that his "good stuff" was hooking her into believing all the lies of the disease again. Jane started getting well when she was able to see the so-called "good stuff" as being part and parcel of the disease. She began to be able to treat it as the disease, no matter what form it took. It was only then that she was able to start getting calm and to deal with what was going on. No matter what came down the pike— whether it was the good "hooking" stuff or the nasty stuff that sent her reeling—she was able to realize where it was actually coming from and to act accordingly.

How can you recognize *true* decent behavior from "hooking" old patterns? By the *results*. If the alcoholic repeatedly woos you, then "zaps" you, he's into "games," again. But changed behavior will be less flamboyant; in a way, humble; and consistently decent.

And, don't expect yourself (and don't let him expect you) to not flinch, for months, when you expect old patterns. If he *really* changes, you'll naturally, in time, not expect to get hurt.

"My grace is sufficient for you, for power is perfected in weakness." (2 Cor. 12:9, NAB).

Write On:

1. "I don't want to deal at all with this idea that his 'good stuff' might be manipulative. It's too depressing."

2. "If I learn to give up immediate gratification (in the form of his saying 'sweet things' and me loving it, in return for us pretending it's really all okay if he drinks), and if I learn to go for the long-term goal of holding out for a sober, sane life for him (and him not dying of alcoholism), I have a good chance of getting it. And if he doesn't choose it, then I've done what I'm supposed to do to help myself and help him and our children. God will take care of me (and will take care of him too, if he will let Him)."

Suggested Activity:

1. Practice doing *any* thing that you formerly weren't able to do. *Do it one day at a time.* Pick something that would upset you if you had to keep it up for a lifetime, something that you can do *just for today.* This habit will give you the strength to, some day, do what you need to do with the alcoholic, whatever that might be.

6

Carrying Excited Misery
Into Your Next Relationship

Peace
in Love
means Joy.

Lana was married to an alcoholic for many years.
When he finally left, he went through a whole
succession of other women. Then he "went down the
drain," divorced Lana and went away—nobody
knew where he was.

Lana was very upset. After all those years she
began to distrust men. Through treatment and
therapy, however, she was able to learn to stop
distrusting men. She started seeing that there were
many, many decent men in the world. But she did not
think she was capable of choosing to marry a man
who would be good to her. She felt that she would be
tricked, that she would find somebody who would be
superficially nice, but who would prove to be as bad
or worse a mate than she had before. Instead of

facing that again, she thought, she would rather be alone.

But as the years of solitary living went by, she decided, for various reasons, to venture out again and to try to have a relationship. She started going to various places to meet men and her friends would fix her up with people. *Yes,* she sometimes did wind up with a stinker, but for every two stinkers she found a really nice guy. Then she went out with Norman and what happened was unfortunately very typical.

Norman was a widower whose wife had died of cancer. They had been happily married for nearly thirty years and he, very frankly, wanted to be married again. He took Lana out and was obviously enthralled with her. He thought she was a terrific person, and they had some very good times together.

He was very good to her and was always looking to find little things he could do for her. For instance, on their first date, while they were sitting in her living room, talking for a minute, something came up about plugging in some electrical appliance somewhere. She made a comment to the effect that it was hard to find anything in her apartment that worked. She didn't mean anything by it. She was just sort of grumbling. But he, right away, got down on his hands and knees and started looking around all the baseboards in the living room. He told her that she needed a certain number of additional outlets in the wall and how he'd like to install them for her. And it was obvious that there were no strings attached.

He just really liked her and wanted to do things for her. She wasn't used to this kind of behavior.

They went out to a restaurant. She was used to her alcoholic ex-husband being very flirtatious with every female no matter what age, size or shape in order to get her upset. At this restaurant there were some people at an adjoining table who had just come from a dance. The man was in a tuxedo and the woman was wearing a gown. They were taking pictures of each other. Lana knew that Norman was an amateur photographer so she leaned over to him and said, "Oh, you ought to take their picture." The couple overheard her. They turned around and asked if he would take their picture for them, and he agreed. Right after he took their picture, however, the woman became very flirtatious with Norman. Lana became rigid; her back just sort of stood up straight. She had encountered this kind of behavior before.

Her alcoholic husband would have become intimate with this woman. He would have leaned forward, looked in her eyes and held an intimate conversation. He wouldn't have been interested in letting it go too far; he just wanted to come on and feel attractive, no matter at whose expense.

But Norman did not respond in this way. Instead, he became rather cool. He gave the camera back, wished the couple luck and came back and sat at the table. And he did not look at Lana with a "haha!" look in his eye, as her husband would have done.

Norman truly changed the subject—in his voice, his mind and his heart. He dropped the whole thing and went on to talk to her animatedly about what they had been talking about before.

Lana was sure that he was sincere. She dated him a few more times and he continued to demonstrate this straight, non-game-playing behavior. He continued to be very good to her. And Lana became very, very upset. She started to say to herself that she was bored with him, that somehow she just could not get excited about him. In therapy she started to realize that the old hooking that always got her very "involved" when she was dating an alcoholic just wasn't there in this relationship with Norman. Therefore, some of the excitement wasn't there either. She wasn't able to resolve this, and had to break up with him. After this she went through a relationship with someone who was not very good to her and she broke up with him too.

There were no roller-coaster ups and downs; Norman had not seemed "terrific," nor was he rotten. He had been just plain nice. More important, he didn't seem *powerful*—and that "power" (albeit over *her,* used as a club) wasn't there. Therefore, Norman seemed "milksoppy."

She started taking her therapy and her Al-Anon more seriously—what actually happened was that she started seeing that life was too short to waste time playing around with old, sick ideas—and she started to really believe that if she did what was good for her, then her mind would follow. That meant that if she started going out with somebody who was very good to her and acted as if she was enjoying the relationship, her mind would catch up and she could start enjoying that person.

She met a widower who was a corporate executive and they started going out together. The man was consistently good to her. He was a regular kind of person who wanted a regular kind of relationship, and she was able to start enjoying that.

Now, at times, she found that she was bringing what her Al-Anon sponsor called "excited misery" into the relationship. Lana started finding that when there was no reason to focus on him for problems (as was the case in her alcoholic marriage), she found that she had to start seeing where her *own* problems were. One of these was that she did not know how to live very comfortably with peace. She had spent a lot of time in her alcoholic marriage counseling her husband, making sure he was doing the right thing, taking care of him, advising him, going into each other's soul's problems and needs. But that was, for the most part, absent in her new relationship. And the relationship seemed shallow to her for this reason.

What did they talk about? They talked about their plans for the day, or made plans about buying something in the future. But, for the most part, there was not the deep soul connection every time they spoke. She felt that something was missing. She thought that she felt a lack of intimacy. She realized that, for the most part, her healthy friends all had relationships like that, in which nobody did heavy counseling all night with their spouses and, except in times of deep crisis, did not expect it. Very few problems were deeply discussed *all* the time.

The house was relatively quiet. And it seemed strange. It seemed like they just weren't very close. She talked to her new husband about this, and he seemed quite puzzled by what she was saying. He didn't see anything wrong with what was going on; he indicated that he was quite happy and quite content with the relationship.

I talked with Lana about this. I told her that I thought that when you start to get peace in the home there is less stress—and perhaps less talk. There is almost no soul-searching and the people just live and let live, and go on about the business of living, instead of talking about living. She thought about that and realized that the latter was exactly what she was doing when she lived with her alcoholic husband. She talked a lot about what he should do and he never did it; she thought and talked a lot about what she was going to do and never did. There just wasn't time and energy to go ahead and do things after you sit up all night and talk about them every night. In *this* marriage, on the other hand, she was going ahead and living her life and her husband was doing the same. They were being peaceful, calm, ethical and good towards themselves, other people and each other. The relationship was basically good and they didn't need to talk about it too much. She was at one point wondering when she was going to give up that sadness or if she ever would give it up. She missed that intimacy, in spite of the fact that the intimacy had come with a price tag: craziness.

At times she found herself stirring up stuff from her past. When her sister, who was still married to a drinking alcoholic, would find herself drawn into the "crazinesses" with her husband, Lana would go visit her. While she was there she would get into that relationship with them and really get into it like she used to, instead of realizing that it wasn't any of her business. For a while she'd be back down there again, full of a kind of soap-opera excitement. Then she would come home to her peaceful house and bring all this junk with her. She would talk about it incessantly, and go on and on and on, involving everybody in the house in her in-law problem. Then she would start to get a headache like she used to and wonder what was going on and why everything was all messed up again.

She didn't realize that she could just turn it down. She could visit her sister if she wanted to—understanding that she was walking into a hornet's nest —and try to put a kind of bubble of protection around herself. She could refrain from offering advice about what her sister should and should not do. She could be compassionate, kind and decent, but at the same time remain sort of detached. She could think about other things when in danger of getting overexcited and overinvolved. She could cut the visit short in a kind way.

When she left her sister's house the next time, she planned to do exactly that. And what she did, to try and calm down before she went home, was to go to a corner soda fountain, order a milk shake and sit with a magazine and just look at some ads for a while. It calmed her down and got her mind off of those excited miseries and thoughts. Then she went home and avoided talking with her husband and children about the whole sordid mess.

There were times when she really did miss the excited misery, but for the most part she learned to want it less and less. Then she realized that she was no longer having the upset stomachs and headaches and that it was actually getting to be quite fun to have some peace. As a matter of fact, she found out that, now that she was at home in a peaceful household, she was able to direct her creative energies towards starting a small, part-time business in her home. She came to like the long-term payoff of her choice very much indeed.

"First keep the peace within yourself, then you can also bring peace to others." (Thomas á Kempis)

Write On:

1. "When I am in a bad relationship, I say to myself, 'If I could only get out of this, I'd settle for anyone who was *decent*.' And then, when I'm dating, men who are always nice bore me. They seem like doormats. They aren't exciting at all."

or:

2. "I've been married to an alcoholic for a long time, and I can't imagine being bored by peace. Me? Never!"

Suggested Activity:

When with friends, practice gently changing the subject to a joyful and hopeful one whenever they bring up misery-laden subjects that they always dwell on. This will help you to relearn how to live with peace and enable you to maximize your areas of recovery.

7

Being Good to Yourself Is Your Quickest and Best Therapy

Be good to yourself.
It gets easy to do, the more you do it.
Not being good to yourself brings on depression,
which brings on physical illnesses.
In the long run, it's cheaper than doctor bills.

You know, in my earlier book, *Getting Them Sober, Volume One,* I included a line which says, in effect, "Be good to yourself—*that's not such a terrible thing for you to have to do, is it?"* A friend of mine, who has never lived with alcoholism, read the book and, in a very puzzled way, asked me why in the world I would ever write a thing like that. I told her that I thought that being good to yourself is one of the most difficult things the spouse of an alcoholic has to do for themselves in therapy and in getting well.

I've counseled many people who've been in Al-Anon

for many years and who do a lot of things very, very well. They are very much together in a lot of ways, can learn to quickly detach and to do quite a lot of necessary things. They don't look like somebody who's just coming into Al-Anon and feeling very bad about themselves. They dress properly, keep a good home and their husbands can be sober in AA for quite a few years. Nevertheless, they're having problems.

When a person like this comes to me, I usually find that if I say, "Why don't you try doing this or that," they'll do it. But the problem comes when I say, "Okay, now we're going to work on you being good to yourself. What are you doing to be good to yourself?" I ask. "What are you doing for fun?" I make it clear that I am not referring to cooking, cleaning, or finding a better way to save money by sewing clothes. Doing something that anyone would consider total relaxation—fun, rest and recuperation. But when I bring this topic up, such people start to squirm.

I talked to a woman who has a moderately decent income and who loves fashionable clothing. I said, "Did you ever think of going to such-and-such a store where I know that they have the fashion magazines from all over Europe? When was the last time you treated yourself to something like that? I know you'd just love it." And she looked at me oddly.

I find that people balk most in the area of taking time for themselves. I counsel some women married to alcoholics who have a great deal of money and I find that they spend most of their time doing things for others. I suggested to one woman what she might do. We ran down a list of things that she did during a typical week and it seemed as if she was spending most of her time either going to therapy or Al-Anon, and cooking and cleaning and being good to every-body else. Consequently, she was distraught, easily upset and beset with a kind of chronic, low-level depression; nothing really appealed to her. She couldn't understand why she couldn't feel real good. So we talked about ways in which she could find more time for herself.

I really think she would have been happier if I would have suggested that she double up on her housework so she could have an extra bit of time. Instead, I suggested, since she certainly could afford it, that she go out and hire a cleaning lady to come in once a week to do the floors, the bathrooms, the laundry and the ironing. In response, this woman looked absolutely upset with me. I further suggested very strongly that she buy a paper cup dispenser and put it in her kitchen and that she also stock up on paper plates for those nights when she didn't feel like doing the dishes, or for those lunches where she just grabs a sandwich and really doesn't want to be bothered by washing up. I also told her that she should feel free to forget about cooking dinner on some nights and just send out for pizza or subs. She was upset by all of this.

I knew that she couldn't be upset because of the money involved. I wanted to show her that her fear was based on something other than the money. So we tallied up how much everything we had been talking about would cost. We discovered that, at most, we were talking about thirty-five to forty dollars a week; that was all. But even though she saw the absurdity of objecting to my suggestions on the grounds of inadequate money she was still very upset and didn't know why.

We explored this further. She finally told me that she couldn't figure out what her reason for existing would be if she didn't wash the cups and plates and do all the housework. I suggested that she *already* was a good wife. I told her that there were a lot of women who fit into the category of being good wives and who are treated very well by their husbands all the time and who wouldn't, under any circumstances, take *any* abuse—which she had certainly faced. In addition to that, I pointed out that she was a wonderful mother.

But somehow she still felt that she had to continue to try and earn the right to be called a good person. What she found out through therapy was that underneath, she was really afraid that if she didn't do a 200- or 300-percent job in her role of wife and mother, then her husband would say something like, "Oh, what do I need you for?" and walk out on her.

I asked her if she judged other women that harshly. She said that of course she did not and went on to tell me about Mrs. Jones and Mrs. Smith up the street whom she knew very well. Their husbands were very good men and had never had problems with alcohol. Their wives did not work outside the home and they had all the amenities we had been talking about, plus many others. Then I asked if these women were good mothers and she agreed that they were. She said that their children were lovely and that that they loved their mothers, who raised them well. She agreed also that these women were good wives. I then asked why she was judging herself more harshly than she judged them. She didn't know why. She didn't even realize how harshly she had been judging herself and trying to continually prove herself a good wife and mother.

We talked about that and about the fact that she was the grown daughter of an alcoholic—how, when young, she had never really been treated for this lack of self-esteem. We talked about how this need to prove oneself comes from being the child of an alcoholic. Such children grow up and often marry alcoholics and are driven to continue to prove, prove, prove. And then we talked about how she had to start dropping this behavior because it was doing nothing but transforming her into a martyr. I told her that it would not get her brownie points and wouldn't get her into heaven. What it did was to keep her sick and neurotic. Worse than that, her "sick" kind of martyrdom was a bad example for her children. I told her that if she couldn't give herself permission to break away from martyrdom and be good to herself, *for* herself, then she should do it for her children. Those kind of martyred, neurotic behavior patterns, I told her, were patterns they learn, to marry alcoholics and/or become alcoholics themselves.

She then started seeing the wisdom of changing her behavior and she started to *want* to do more. Then she said, "Well, while I still have these irrational guilt feelings, what do I do?"

"It's not a matter of *thinking* your way into good living—you have to *live* your way into good thinking. This means that, okay, you have these feelings—so what? Start acting as if you don't have these feelings and acting *as if* you're healthy. No matter how you feel, once you get the body in gear, your mind is eventually going to catch up.

"You have to start off small. You start buying the paper plates and cups and it will soon feel so good to be able to throw things out instead of having to wash dishes over and over again. One night a week, when you really don't feel like cooking, but still—of course—want to serve your family a balanced meal, you send out for subs with lettuce and tomatoes. They provide the nutrients your family needs. Then you expand from there. Start pampering yourself in these small ways and, believe me, you'll start liking it. Your guilt will go out the window as you start doing these sorts of things. You'll get healthier and will set a good example for your children. They'll learn from you how really healthy anti-alcoholic ways of living can be. And your husband, after his initial anger,

Write On:

1. (Complete this sentence): "I'm more comfortable buying for others than myself because _____

_____

_____

_____

_____ ."

2. Describe the life, as you see it, of one woman whom you know well and like—someone who pampers herself.

3. Would God punish that woman for pampering herself? Why, or why not?

Suggested Activity:

Write out all of your reasons for postponing pampering yourself. Then carefully reread this chapter. After you reread the chapter, write down why your original reasons don't hold water.

could be certain that he's sincere about wanting to stay sober.

First, it is important to realize that no one can know another person's motives. You're not going to be able to read your husband's mind dispassionately, even if you're good at it. Then, even if he stays sober, don't expect too much of yourself. It takes a long time—not just a few weeks or months—for him to reconstruct the trust you had in him at one time, a long time ago.

I know a woman who has been through treatment in Al-Anon for her family alcoholism for many years; her husband has been sober for many years too. They have a good relationship now. She told me that when he first got sober she had been through so many false alarms—ten of them, as a matter of fact—that it took her a full year before she could even sit on the same sofa with him. Not next to him, but just on the other end of the sofa. So don't expect that your trust in him will return right away, even though he may expect it to do so. He may come home from the detox center and say, "Well, what's wrong with you. You're looking at me like you don't trust me. I've been sober for three days now." But that's not enough to build trust in anyone. Three years, yes. Three days, no.

You do not have to accept the guilt that he is trying to make you feel. He's still "crazy." Just because he's been out of a treatment center for a few days or been dry for a similar period does not mean that he's sober. There's a big difference between *dry* and *sober*. Sober means having a normally decent outlook on life, treating the family well, practicing the twelve steps of AA on a reasonably regular basis and so forth. Dry is when you get the booze out of your system.

So, back to the question of your spouse's sincerity. How can you know if he's sincere or not? Well, since you can't judge his motives, what you *can* look at are his *actions*. Not what he says, not what he feels. He's going to feel rotten while he's going through acute withdrawal. What are his actions? Is he going to at least one AA meeting every day? I don't care what else he's saying or what excuses he's giving. Is he going to ninety AA meetings in ninety days after he gets out of the treatment center? That's the kind of thing you should look for.

Now, if he's been ordered to go to AA by a court or by his boss, or even because you've told him that you won't take him back unless he goes, okay. Let's see his behavior in another area too. Is he going to more than just the minimum required number of AA meetings? After he's been going to AA for a few months it should have sunk in—that is, if he's going to stay sober—that AA is where his health is. I would say that he's on his way to good sobriety if he's going to extra meetings on a regular basis to get help for particularly rough days, even though he doesn't *have* to, according to the judge, his boss or you.

A very good indication that he's going to stay sober this time is whether or not he's taking pills.

A non-psychotic, sober alcoholic should not be on any mind-altering drugs. No tranquilizers, pot, sleeping pills, etc. If he is, he's simply eating his booze. It's all the same disease—"sedativism."

You're probably thinking about one or two things right now. Either he is doing what's right and you're feeling scared that he's going to stop, or he's *not* doing what he's supposed to and you have no idea what to do next.

Let's take the first situation first. What if he has thrown himself into treatment and is doing what he's supposed to do? You're understandably wondering how you can know if he's going to keep it up. You can't. Nobody can. And it's normal and natural that you feel scared. Go to Al-Anon, or get extra counseling; it's very important for you, if you are to be able to calm down and take life one day at a time, to get help at this point. You need a support system which understands you and which will help you to get through this period, *no matter what he does or doesn't do.*

It is also important to remember at this time that it's necessary for you to keep part of yourself out of this situation and not bank too much on expectations that he will stay sober. I know how badly you want him to do so. But it's not good for you to want this *too badly. It keeps you small and him big.* If he sees that you bank on him so much, that you put him way up there on that pedestal as some kind of tin god, it's not good for his sobriety. And it's not good for *your getting well. That's* more important for *you.* The bigger you make him, the more important you make him and what he does, and the less important you're making yourself. The less important you make yourself, the more vulnerable you feel about yourself.

That's not the reality. *You are really not that vulnerable.* It's just that you think you are vulnerable; the more you think yourself vulnerable, the more you act vulnerable, and so on. It's a vicious circle. And the more vulnerable you feel and act, the greater the chance there is for him to get the upper hand and to hurt you emotionally.

How do you stop panic and despair? Let's assume that you will go to Al-Anon or counseling. You'll get the support that is necessary for you, especially at Al-Anon. One of the things you can do is to use one of those good AA slogans: "You can't think your way into good living; you have to live your way into good thinking." That means that when you go to a healing Al-Anon session, or a therapy session, on a *regular* basis, the healing will take place—you *will* get better—despite any self-sabotaging you may do. However, your healing will speed up if you start taking action before your mind says you're ready. In other words, if you start acting in very small ways *as if* you are not worried about whether he gets sober and stays sober, then you will become peaceful.

Now I know it's hard. I can imagine you would feel that if you don't act as if you're worried, and if you wind up *not* worried, then he's going to get drunk again. Well, it really doesn't matter how you act. If he wants to get drunk or stay sober, he's going to get drunk or stay sober. If that man has a sincere desire to stay sober, he's going to stay sober even if you hit him over the head every day with a brick. He's going to stay sober whether you're nice or not—if *he wants* to stay sober.

An alcoholic will do what he wants to do, just like everybody else. So, if he's going to do what *he* wants to do, no matter what *you* do, where does that leave you? It leaves you holding the bag of your own feelings about him. So the only thing to do is to *act as if* you are not emotionally concerned with the outcome of his attempts at sobriety, so that *you* get well and stop getting depressed, and stop getting headaches and stomach problems.

This can be done in small ways. You will know when those small ways come up. When family members engage you in conversation about whether or not he's really going to stay sober, you can murmur noncommittally and change the subject. If they do not accept your changing the subject, you can walk away. Also, when you get the worrying thoughts in your mind you can say, "Nope. I'm not going to worry about this now. I'll worry about it later—say, three o'clock." Then, if you start to worry at five o'clock you can tell yourself that you're not allowed to worry until three o'clock the next day.

Why worry now? It doesn't get you any answers; it

does absolutely no good; it gets you nowhere. All it does is to stop you from being happy and productive in the very present, right now.

I know it's hard to do, but when you think about all the possible things that could happen, there really isn't any other answer. He's going to do what he's going to do, no matter what you do. If you could have stopped him from drinking or could have made him sober, it would have happened a long time ago. If he's getting sober now, for real, he's doing it because he really *wants* to. The motivation might be there. If it's not enough of a motivation, he's not going to follow through, that's all. It's really that simple. It has nothing to do with whether or not you watch him and make sure that he's staying away from the booze.

True, that can work for a little while. But it doesn't work forever. At some point, if he's doing it, he's going to be staying sober because *he* wants to. And no person has enough energy to live his own life *and* keep his own head spiritually and mentally above water *and* still push and cajole another person enough to get them to go to treatment *and* make sure that they stay sober. If you spend all of your time doing that, you're going to go down the tubes emotionally. You're going to be the one who gets the anxiety attacks, the stomach aches and the back pains. You will fall apart. You cannot keep your life and run *his* at the same time. So the only thing you can do is to *try* to let go, and let God.

And how will you know if he's sincere? You'll see it,

on a daily basis, by whether or not he stays sober. Only time is going to tell. If he stays dry for months and then eventually proceeds to real sobriety, you will see it.

Now, if you're separated from him and you ask how long you should stay away to make sure that he is going to really stay sober, I'd say six months to a year if you can manage it. If you've stayed away, or made him stay away, and if you see that he's not sincere in his efforts to stay sober, unfortunately, I would say then that he will probably get drunk. In that case, you should go back to step one and deal with him as if he were a drinking alcoholic, during which time your expectations were not so high. But do whatever you have to do to survive yourself. I would not, however, get your hopes up if this man is not following a *daily* sobriety program of some kind.

This does not have to be a depressing time of life for you. A lot of people in AA slip, in early sobriety, and many make numerous attempts at getting sober before they actually succeed at it.

Try to look at this as if you're just taking inventory of a situation. If you owned a grocery store and times were tough, you would just go through and do an inventory. If the peas and carrots weren't moving, you'd get rid of them. If you were selling a lot of lima beans, you'd stock up on more of them. You'd be tough in your inventory and you'd take it down to the bare bones.

So, in assessing the situation, to pretend that some-

Fact:

It takes a very long time—often years—without "slips" and emotional battering to stop being distrustful of the alcoholic's behavior. If he is dry for just months, and he becomes angry with you for "not trusting him," suggest that he read the chapter called "The Family Afterward" in The Big Book called *Alcoholics Anonymous*. It talks about how an alcoholic's getting sober is like coming up out of a storm cellar after a typhoon has destroyed the house. He may be happy that the "storm" has stopped, but he doesn't look around to see the damage that will take a long, long time to repair.

Write On:

The ways in which you possibly see the alcoholic as important—those ways that are essentially detrimental to your well-being.

Suggested Activity:

Write down a few small ways in which you could imagine doing things that would whittle away at the alcoholic's excessive importance to you. Do one of them this week.

9

If It's Good for You,
It's Good for Him

Taking is good, healthy medicine for you.

Giving to his family is healthy medicine for the alcoholic.

Your disease wants you to feel guilty about taking.

I once heard a very wise woman say that the alcoholic's main problem is his involvement with himself. For him to get well he has to get out of himself and learn to give, not only to other alcoholics, but also to his family. If the recovering alcoholic wants to get well, he will give of his time to other alcoholics and to his family. In *early* sobriety, he will learn how to give by working with other alcoholics.

That is probably true during early sobriety. But after a year or two of sobriety, I think it's reasonable and justifiable that the alcoholic's family tell him that it is time for him to start to give to *them*; that he should take *some* of the time that he has been putting into AA and into helping other alcoholics and spend it with his family. This does not mean that he must cut back on his meetings. He can go to a meeting every day, arranging his schedule so that some of his time remains available for his family. An arrangement of this sort is rarely impossible.

This may inconvenience him. He may have to get up an hour or so earlier, but if he is serious about wanting to spend some time with his wife and children during the evening, then he will not regard this as much of a sacrifice.

There's a very important reason why the alcoholic should spend some time with his family. In effect, it's a more humble kind of giving than giving to other alcoholics. There's more ego involved in going out and doing the twelve-step call and helping another alcoholic, or doing things at AA meetings to help others than it is to come home and spend some time going over Suzy's spelling or Billy's reading or listening to them talk about their day.

On the other hand, if the non-alcoholic spouse is going to get well, she is going to have to learn to take. That is probably the hardest thing that the non-alcoholic spouse must learn to do. It makes even those who are almost completely well squirm sometimes. It's hard for the alcoholic to learn how to give joyfully without resentment, and it's very hard for the non-alcoholic to learn how to take joyfully without guilt.

If it's good for you, it's good for him. If you're

taking, in the sense of doing what's good for you—not for anyone else—then it's good. If it pampers you, if it makes you feel good, it's good for you. And if it's good for you, it means that you are centered on yourself, not him; he's centered on you, and his giving and your taking is extremely good for his sobriety. *If you can't do it at first, if you can't joyfully take without guilt, then it's a good idea to take for his sake. It will be good for his sobriety in the long run.*

If you're feeling like something is wrong, like this is too good to be true and it seems almost sinful, try to remember that *that guilt is your disease talking. And if your alcoholic gets angry, resentful and depressed that he has to give, give, give after all those years of take, take, take, that's his disease talking. And if you don't start taking and he doesn't start giving, the result is that you are perpetuating the disease within your entire family.* As a result, your children will learn these behavior patterns; when they grow up, they stand a good chance of becoming and/or marrying alcoholics. Therefore, if you want to stop this disease in your family, do some taking *even if it doesn't feel good.* Get the body there and the mind will follow. It's healthy for you to take at least 50 percent of the time. There *will* come a time when you will learn to feel good about it.

I don't doubt that you are giving more than 50 percent of the time. It's very rare to find a spouse of an alcoholic who's not giving most of the time. That's the unhealthy part. That unhealthy continual giving which is not really giving is one of the cores of the disease. Underneath it all is a lot of resentment. That's normal and natural; but the only way to clear up the resentment, to feel good about yourself and lose that bitterness towards him, is to start taking. And if you feel so angry that you do not want to give up that bitterness, well, try to think it through.

It may feel good at the moment to feel bitter and to hold on to that anger, but it doesn't really feel good in the long run. It may be normal and natural to feel that way, but in the long run you're going to be a happier person—within yourself, about yourself and for yourself—if you can learn to take.

Turning down gifts from him is not healthy, regardless of what his motives are. If he's done something rotten and he gives you a gift afterwards, take it. You don't have to feel good about what he did. Take the gift and run. If he brings you something because he feels good and he wants to make you happy, take it. Learn to do the taking. That will raise your self-esteem more than anything else that you can do.

You've got to raise your self-esteem. The quickest way to do it is to take—it's part and parcel of being good to yourself. And even if you don't care whether or not it's good for him, even if you want to get back at him, it doesn't matter. The important thing is *you* and *your getting well.* And, as a by-product, he just might get well if you get well. Also, it decreases his guilt if you take more because underneath all that

Write On:

List the ways in which you might feel that it's wrong or uncomfortable, for you to be taking, instead of giving, at least 50 percent more than you do now.

Suggested Activity:

Make two notes on an index card, to carry in your purse, to look at during those times when you feel guilty about taking instead of always giving, giving, giving. The first note should say, "THAT'S YOUR DISEASE TALKING" and the second should say, "IF IT'S GOOD FOR YOU, IT'S GOOD FOR HIM."

10

Verb-Love Versus Noun-Love

*As your self-esteem rises, as you go to Al-Anon,
you won't need just pretty words.*
*As you get healthier, the alcoholic will respect you
more.*

The alcoholic hears what you *do* and not what you
say; the spouse of the alcoholic hears what the
alcoholic *says* and not what he *does*.

Let's think about that for a minute. How many
times does the spouse of an alcoholic threaten the
alcoholic with angry statements like, "I'm not going
to take this any more. I'm going to leave"? How
many times is the spouse of an alcoholic reduced to
yelling, screaming, pleading, counseling, staying up
all night, telling him how to lead his life so that he will
get well, will stop hurting you, will stop spending his
whole paycheck at a bar, will get sober? But what
happens? After he agrees with you, he goes right out
and starts drinking again.

The alcoholic does not hear what you say. He hears

what you do. This is not a conscious act on his part. The alcoholic does not say to himself, "I'm not going to listen to anything she says because she doesn't really mean it." He simply knows from experience that he can just let you talk and yell and scream and sulk and cry, but that it doesn't mean anything. He knows that you're going to stay no matter what you say. He knows that if he just hangs in there, he can continue with his irresponsible behavior.

On the other hand, the spouse of the alcoholic does not really pay attention to what the alcoholic does, only what he says. It's only when he says, "I love you" that she listens, takes in what he says. As long as the alcoholic tells his spouse that he loves her, that she is special to him and important, a good woman who puts up with him even though he doesn't deserve it, and that he will never leave her, it doesn't seem to matter what he does.

I know a woman who has been separated from her alcoholic husband for almost thirty years. He left her almost thirty years ago and now lives about five states away. But he still sends her Christmas cards and calls her every year. He pops in her life once in a great while to tell her that he loves her, and she thinks that they have a marriage. She pays no attention at all to what he does; she only hears what he says. She's living in a very starved way for that occasional expression of "love."

Noun-love versus verb-love. He doesn't have to *do* love: he just has to *say* it. That's the way your alcoholic, in his sickness, hooks you into staying with him. All the sweet words cost him nothing, and he gets to keep on the way he has been living for years and years, and he gets you to stay with him in the bargain.

There is a way to stay in that marriage, if you so choose, without being hooked. But if you choose to stay, (just for today, since no one knows where they'll be five months from now), there are ways to avoid being trapped in that noun-love versus verb-love situation. Keep reminding yourself what the actual reality is; put a sign on your coffee table that says, "Remember the Facts."

The fact is that he has a disease called alcoholism. Some of the symptoms of that disease are that he is unconsciously going to try and hook you into feeling guilt, pity, rage and worry so that you will rescue him, take care of his disease, and help him, in effect, to continue dying from his disease. Therefore, you have to realize that when you want to rescue him, *you're not rescuing your husband, you're really rescuing his disease.* And when his disease wants you to get into all kinds of neurotic feelings in order to help it to continue to live, you have to tell yourself that it's just the disease talking. If you tell yourself that, then you'll be able to reject the disease. You'll be able to differentiate it from your husband. If you say "no" to your husband, it can bring on all kinds of guilt feelings. But if you say "no" to a disease, it's quite okay; in fact, it's necessary.

Saying "no" to a disease—*seeing* that it's the disease—is a way to divorce yourself from the hooking, neurotic feelings that stop you from acting and living out your own life happily and fruitfully while he works out his problem.

If he doesn't recognize the disease as his own then he can't do anything about it. If his disease has become your property, if you have taken on his disease, he won't be able to deal with it; it's in *your* hands, and not in his, where it belongs. If you give it back to him, and he stands there holding it, then he can begin to do something about it.

So when he gives you that noun-love as opposed to verb-love, tell yourself that it's just the disease talking and trying to get you to save it, to prolong its existence. Respond by refusing to help that disease, despite its loving words.

"They that wait upon the Lord shall renew their strength; they shall mount up with wings as eagles; they shall run, and not be weary; and they shall walk, and not faint." (Isa. 40:31)

Write On:

Specific instances where you may have placed too much importance on what people said, instead of shrugging it off.

Suggested Activities:

1. Try to stop yourself from saying "I love you" so often to the alcoholic.

2. When you're at work or with friends, try to ask yourself, "How important is it?" when someone says something annoying.

11

Nothing Makes You Feel Crazier Than Sexual Games

He is "playing games."
You are okay.
Go and be with people who accept you as you are.

Let me describe a typical scenario. Everything seems to be going all right. You're sitting in your living room, reading your newspaper. He's watching a football game on television. All of a sudden, out of the clear blue sky, he looks at you, makes a comment, and gives you "a look." On the surface, the comment seems to be quite normal. But somehow it triggers something in you. It enrages you. You know he's "doing it again." He's doing something to puff himself up at your expense. And it's about another woman.

What makes you feel so crazy or so enraged is that *you know he really doesn't care about this woman.* He could be talking about a woman who is forty years his senior, but it's just like comments he's made before about this kind of thing. It's more of the groundwork he has been laying over a certain period of time. It's the look he gives you that says, "Aha, I have you this time, don't I?" It's all done in a flash, and you blow up and get furious even though you realize that there is no way he could be attracted to this person, and that he's only trying to get you upset.

Then you show your anger, and say something like, "There you go, you're doing it again."

He replies, "Doing what?" *That's the trap.* You sort of stumble around, knowing full well what's coming, knowing inherently that you're not crazy, that what you are saying is really true and really going on. But what happens?

He says, "That's crazy" or "You're crazy" or both. And he may go on to tell you to go to a "shrink," and may even threaten to leave you if you "keep it up." So you tell him to go ahead and he storms off and starts packing. But by the time he gets to the door you're ready to ask him to stay. Then he says, "I'll stay only if you'll stop this craziness." Then he triumphantly sticks around and you get depressed *because you know what really went on.*

Trudi's story reflects a more intricate problem, albeit a similar one. She had been married to a man who was mentally very cruel to her. After her divorce she started to go out steadily with a man who had, so to speak, a lower profile than her husband had. *His* "junk" came out only every two or three weeks, although it was rather regular.

When he was normal-acting, he was quiet and decent; that was the face that the world generally saw. When he wanted distance (and he was used to it; he had been living basically alone for years, and was really afraid of the vulnerability that intimacy made possible) he attacked Trudi's "jugular." After a while, Trudi learned that in order to avoid this problem, she had to avoid intimacy with him. It seemed to work; he didn't seem to mind. In fact, much of the time he seemed to take pleasure in being left alone.

But often, when Trudi would want them to share, he would push her away. She would find herself again facing his "junk." Then, when she screamed that he was "doing it again," he would deny that he had done anything. He would tell her that she was crazy and jealous and that he wasn't going to put up with her "way of living in confrontation." Over and over again he threatened to leave her, unless she promised not to bring up subjects that he didn't want to hear about—namely, her insistance that she wasn't crazy, and that he was, in fact, doing all those things to get her angry and that she wasn't inherently jealous (which she in fact knew to be the case.)

When he sometimes carried out his threat of leaving her, by going over to another drinking alcoholic's house, she wanted him back because, as she said, "It was more pleasant to have him around if only I could pretend that nothing was ever wrong.

Besides, he isn't as vicious as my husband was."

But there was a high price to pay. She had to call him and beg him to come home, and then he would tell his drunk friends that he'd go back if only she'd stop acting so jealous. They'd all support him in his "macho junk" and never question his behavior. (Actually, he may have wanted her to become jealous because he was basically so insecure himself.)

If you try to explain it to anybody who has not lived with that kind of craziness, they'll think you're crazy. This is because they cannot imagine that kind of craziness. Even if you try to explain it to a helping professional, they may not know what you are talking about. Many professionals don't know of that particular kind of alcoholic crazy-making; they've never seen it or experienced it and they've never read about it in the literature. As a result, they think that maybe you're exaggerating.

Well, if it were a one-shot thing, if it only happened once or twice, then you would be exaggerating. But when it happens often—once every few days, once every week or two weeks, or once a month—over a period of years, there's an erosion that occurs in your self-esteem. You feel less sexually attractive. You get sensitized to this kind of battering. When it happens you get, of course, very upset.

Other people who don't live with it don't understand. But if you live with it, you know that it's really going on. When you go to Al-Anon and share this, you will find a lot of women who are living in the same kind of situation. Not all alcoholics are like this, but *many* of them are.

It is a part of alcoholism that is not talked about much in the literature. *But it's one of the most enraging, depressing, crazy-making characteristics of alcoholic behavior.*

What helps to make you realize that you are not unique or crazy is to go to Al-Anon and share this. There you will find other women who will tell you that they have been through, or are going through, the same kind of situation. This will help you to realize that this kind of behavior is part of a general pattern.

This is unconscious behavior, and the alcoholic often doesn't even know what he's doing. This is not to say that such behavior is not hurtful to you. Whether or not he knows what he's doing doesn't matter awfully much. But when he is feeling bad about himself, the behavior of setting you up, knocking you down and puffing himself up at your expense often temporarily relieves his depression. Then he doesn't have to deal with the real reason for his own depression, nor with himself and where his life is going.

A woman I know named Sally told me that her husband would not use this kind of behavior with the really attractive women she knew. He instinctively knew that if he did react to women who in *her* opinion were attractive, she would not get upset. She would say to herself, and to him, "Well, of course you find her attractive. She's beautiful. She really is." She would sort of shrug it off like that and his tactic would become totally ineffective. As a result, he would become more depressed. But if he used someone who was less attractive than she, he could trigger feelings of insecurity in her that made her feel less than good about herself. That was exactly his purpose.

Now, if you can tell yourself that you know what he's doing and that he really doesn't even think this other women is attractive and is just using that to get you mad, that can help to relieve some of your feelings of inadequacy.

It *doesn't* help your anger. You want him to stop this behavior. One way you can stop him is by looking at him as if you are on top of the situation. Just act as if you are on top, and grin at him as if to say, "Ha, I've got you. You don't have me." Do that enough times and you'll start to know and believe that you *are* on top of the situation. Nothing has to be—or should be—spoken to him about this. Just do it. And then, with your head up and a knowing grin—even though you don't feel it—change the subject and keep the smile. He will then lose that puffed-up, air-balloon expression right before your eyes. Do this frequently enough, and eventually he's going to stop that behavior.

It may take awhile. He may continue to do it. But after a while he will drop that behavior. You will probably see an increase in his depression, but at least he has to deal with his disease and *you* don't. And you will see an increase in your self-esteem. You will start to see the truth about this real disease and about your husband. When he abandons this type of behavior you will find that there was no basis to it, that the whole thing was a paper tiger in the first place, that it really had nothing to do with who and what you are.

"No one can make you feel inferior without your consent." (Eleanor Roosevelt)

Write On:

1. Write down all the compliments you can remember having received from family and friends about your overall attractiveness as a person and as a woman.

2. Write down the sincere statements your alcoholic has made, at times, about your attractiveness (when he wasn't acting crazy).

Suggested Activities:

1. Look at yourself when you look very good and write an objective "report" on how good you look.

2. If you've been dressing only in dark colors, but something in shocking pink or another bright color looks great on you—wear it.

3. Dress up, even when you're going to be "just by yourself."

12

If Your Alcoholic Spouse
—or Someone Else—
Says That *You* Have a Drinking
and/or Pill Problem

Be good to yourself, in the highest sense.
Don't let your feelings towards him stop you from
getting well yourself.

I'd like to tell Jody's story. Jody is married to a
bright, highly respected, but drinking alcoholic man.
She went to Al-Anon and to counseling off and on,
but never really seriously threw herself into the
program of getting well herself. She thought she was
doing a good job of detaching and in several sessions
spoke contemptuously of her husband. We talked
about that, about how it was really not in her long-
term best interest to maintain a feeling of superiority
towards her alcoholic husband because, whether or
not she stayed with him, it would hinder her growth
as a person. To maintain that stance would make her

ultimately unhappy. I agreed of course that it is very easy to feel contemptuous toward an alcoholic we're involved with. It's probably one of the most natural feelings in the world, one of the defenses that we use to separate ourselves from the alcoholic's life style. And it feels nicer than feeling pure, unadulterated hatred for him.

One night, during a particularly vitriolic argument, her alcoholic husband accused Jody of having a drinking problem. He pointed out that her parents had a drinking problem too. She became very insulted and told him "to go take a flying leap." Her husband, whose drinking problem was worse than hers, felt very insulted by her too. So, instead of going to AA when he was dry for a few days, he started regularly attending Al-Anon—more frequently than *she* did. He didn't tell her about this, he just started going. One night she walked into her Al-Anon meeting and found him sitting there. He looked at her rather smugly. She became very angry and humiliated and walked out.

About two months later, as this continued, they separated and he moved across town. Periodically, when he would call her about working out certain situations in the household, he let her know that he was continuing to go to Al-Anon meetings. He would "call her" an alcoholic and tell her that the Al-Anon group was praying for her. She became absolutely furious. She got off the phone and called me. I suggested that if he said that again, to take the wind out of his sails by saying, "Thank you. I need all the prayers I can get."

Well, the next time he called her, about two days later (a week or so before our therapy session), he told her again that the Al-Anon group was praying for her. She said exactly what I told her to say. That stopped him dead. He sort of stumbled over his words and mumbled something and got off the phone very quickly.

She recounted this to me when she came in. I suggested that if he did it again she should just thank him and try to sound really surprised and happy that he was praying for her and that he had everybody in Al-Anon praying for her. That would end *that* stuff.

Then I started to talk with her about *her* drinking problem. I said, "Jody, listen. Let's forget about your husband for a minute. Very probably his motives are totally rotten, but, you know, God sometimes speaks to us through strange people. And perhaps, just perhaps, he might have something there in what he's saying." I told her, in fact, that I didn't think that she would become that angry about his accusation if it had no basis in fact whatsoever.

Jody is a very bright woman. She is a computer specialist and known to be quite brilliant in her field. She's a systems analyst, a manager in a systems analyst training and education program, and has her master's degree in mathematics. I reminded her of these things. Then I went on to say, "Listen, Jody, if your husband had accused you of being stupid, professionally stupid, of never getting ahead in your field, you would be incredulous. You wouldn't be able to believe that he was talking like that. You might even be a little alarmed for his sanity, rather than feel angry. In other words, he wouldn't be able to *get* you where you have a small, vulnerable part. He would just seem entirely insane to you. In fact, you might even be compassionate and laugh a little and tell him that he might as well drop it because you don't feel at all inadequate about your intellectual abilities, and there's no way that he's going to be able to make you feel otherwise.

"But you responded angrily to his accusation that you have a drinking problem. I think we ought to look at that.

"Now, before you get angry at me, Jody, and tell me that you don't have a drinking problem, let me say this. Let's not talk about whether your husband is right or wrong. Even if we would find that you are a late-stage alcoholic, *this does not validate your husband one bit*. This does not mean that your husband is right and you are wrong. This does not mean that everything you've said about your marriage is going to be invalid. *This is a separate issue. Even though this is one thing he's said that may have some validity, it does not mean that he can get away with the rotten way he's been behaving towards you and the children.*

"So, if we're going to look at whether you have a problem or not with drinking, let's not confuse the issue. Let's not say that this means that your perception of your relationship is wrong. It doesn't mean that at all. In fact, I think your perception of your relationship has been quite right. But I want to make a very important point here, Jody. If you do have a possible drinking problem, it's extremely important that you treat it and not blind yourself to it *simply because he pointed it out to you.* If you do that, it's called biting off your nose to spite your face.

"Alcoholism is a progressive and fatal disease. I don't think you want to get progressively worse and maybe die or kill somebody on the highway or wind up with a wet brain in the back ward of a mental hospital somewhere, just to prove that your husband is wrong. Your decision about what to do about your alcoholic husband and all the other very rotten things he's done has nothing to do with whether or not you treat a disease that is very treatable. It's a completely separate issue."

I asked Jody how much she drank and she told me. When I asked her if she could stop drinking for a year she looked horrified. She went on to tell me that she could if she wanted to, but why should she? Then she made the classic alcoholic statement. She said, "I can control my drinking."

I went on and asked Jody if it was true that one of her parents was an alcoholic. She indicated that her father "probably" had a drinking problem. We went over the twenty questions of AA and it turned out that she had to answer yes to about eleven of them on her father's behalf. She reluctantly admitted that her father was an alcoholic.

We talked about the disease statistics. I said, "You know, if one of your parents is an alcoholic and you drink, you have at least a 60 percent chance of becoming an alcoholic yourself. If you have two alcoholic parents, then you have close to a hundred percent chance of becoming an alcoholic if you drink."

I went on to talk about the medical symptoms of early-stage alcohol addiction. "One of them," I told her, "is that there is a change in tolerance. If it takes four or five drinks to get the same effect as you used to get from two drinks, that means that your body's alcohol tolerance has changed and that you are physically addicted.

"Now, after your body has *increasing* tolerance for a while, at a later stage of alcoholism, the tolerance changes again—and *decreases*. It then takes very little to get you drunk or high." I asked Jody if she had noticed any change in tolerance in herself. She just looked very morose and nodded her head. Her eyes glinted, she blushed and she got rather angry with me.

"Well," I said, "If you have to give me that kind of answer, you're addicted to alcohol. That means that you're an alcoholic. You're not a stumbling-down drunk, or a skid-row bum. You're a nice woman with a marvelous career and who has a disease that's treatable. I think that if you want to continue having that career and don't want to wind up on skid row or worse, you might want to do something about your drinking."

I am glad to say that Jody is now attending Alcoholics Anonymous and is doing well in her program. She is sober and has gotten two promotions within the past six months. Her work has improved markedly since she got that monkey off her back and got sober.

"God is our refuge and strength, a very present help in trouble." (Ps. 46:1)

Write On:

1. Take the twenty-question test at the back of *Getting Them Sober, Volume One*. You do not have to show the results to your spouse.

2. If you take tranquilizers and wonder if you have an addiction problem with them, ask yourself how you would feel if you could never again take another one. Write about this.

Suggested Activity:

If the prospect of getting off alcohol and/or pills makes you uneasy, that strongly suggests that you have an addiction problem. Consult a physician or other specialist in addictions. To find such a specialist, call the telephone operator and ask for the number of Alcoholics Anonymous. (Alcoholics Anonymous numbers are answered twenty-four hours a day.) Ask the person who answers the phone for the name of a private alcoholism treatment center near you. See them for a consultation.

13

Could You Be Hiding Behind Your Religion?

God accepts me just as I am.
I must learn to accept myself.
Love God, love others, love yourself.

In Alcoholics Anonymous, one of the things that's stressed as being very important for the alcoholic's recovery is his ability to get honest with himself. It's stressed that this does not just mean "cash register" honesty, but honesty about one's motives and what one is really doing and has really done. Only then can the alcoholic get into the twelve steps of AA, part of which is to admit to yourself, to another human being and to God the exact nature of your wrongs. It's very important to talk about the exact nature of your wrongs and then go ahead and "clean house," so to speak.

I've counseled with many women. I'm thinking of one woman in particular who told me that when her husband left, she had gotten the strength, through her Higher Power, to tell her husband, when he told her that he wanted to come home, that he could do so only if he got help. She told him that he needed help for his disease so that she would have a husband, their children would have a father, and so that he wouldn't die. She was very firm. If he refused to get help, she would not allow him to come home.

After this had been going on for about a week, she talked to a woman in her church who knew nothing about alcoholism. This woman told her that, according to her religion, she was wrong in not letting him come home right away, regardless of what he had done. This woman's words made her feel very guilty and, as a result, she let her husband come home.

I talked to her about this and suggested that perhaps she should look at this in two ways. I pointed out that the woman who had talked to her knew absolutely nothing about alcoholism. She did not know that sometimes one way of dealing with alcoholism is to force the alcoholic into treatment. I told her that this woman probably thought it best to treat the alcoholic with tender, loving care as you would the victim of a heart attack. "The problem is," I said, "that this disease is like no other. If you treat an alcoholic the same way you treat a heart attack victim, the alcoholic is quite likely to die from his disease."

Also, they say in AA that you can hide a bad motive

behind a good motive. I strongly suggested further that she look at her own motives. I did not feel that her only motive in letting him back home was guilt. After all, I told her, it always sounds nice to identify a religious motive for one's actions as opposed to a very personal one like, "I was scared to be alone and was worried about money," or "I was afraid that if he stayed out there on the streets he would find someone else and leave me for good."

I told her that the purpose of being absolutely honest with oneself about one's motives is so that you, as a family member, can get well.

The main symptom of alcoholism, the family disease, is denial. Family members grow up expressing denial in all kinds of areas. For instance, a friend of mine just told me that she and her new business partner, a woman who is the grown child of an alcoholic father, went to a family gathering in New York. This business partner's father was at that gathering and he was drunk. He was making a fool of himself, and he was an absolute mess. And everybody pretended that nothing was the matter. Afterwards, when this woman and her new business partner were talking about the party, her business partner said nothing at all about her father's very evident drunkenness, but instead was enthusiastic about the party and how terrific it was to see everybody again. She completely ignored the fact that her father had spent most of his time falling into his food.

The denial mechanism in families of alcoholics is

extremely strong. Alcoholic families don't make mountains out of molehills as often as they make *molehills out of mountains*. That's the denial. If you don't admit that anything bad is going on, then you don't have to deal with it.

The problem is that it doesn't go away. It's going to have to be dealt with at some time or other. If you don't tell yourself that one of your motives for letting him come back too soon, before he gets help, is fear of being alone—*and that's normal*—you'll never get to the point where you can start dealing with that fear of being alone. And if you don't admit to it and start dealing with it, you'll never get past it. But once you start even admitting it to yourself, the problem is half licked.

"It is always easier to believe than to deny." (John Burroughs)

Write On:

1. "I've made mountains out of molehills in the following situations":

2. "I've made molehills out of mountains in the following situations":

Suggested Activity:

Keep a journal of all your feelings, thoughts and actions for one entire day. Write these words beside each entry: "This is fine. God accepts me just as I am."

14

Intervention: Forcing the Alcoholic to Get Sober

Let go and let God determine the outcome.
God loves you.
He understands.

Intervention is the term used by professionals in the field of alcoholism to denote the method by which the alcoholic is boxed into going to treatment. It's done in many ways. One of them is by means of an Employee Assistance Program.

Many major corporations today have Employee Assistance Programs. Some of them deal strictly with alcohol and drug abuse; others have a broader approach and deal with all kinds of mental health problems. Sometimes the family is included in the intervention, sometimes not. In any case, the alcoholic's job performance is noted by the supervisor who is trained in this field. The alcoholic, after a certain process, is referred to a counselor in the

Employee Assistance Program who then, assuming that the alcoholic has been warned about his poor job performance without result, has the power to say to the alcoholic, "You have a choice. Either the company is going to fire you, or you can go to evaluation and treatment."

Many times, alcoholics do not work where there are Employee Assistance Programs, especially if they do not work for large corporations, or in federal, state or local government. Often the alcoholic, in order to escape all kinds of responsibility, will be, so to speak, "self-employed." This often means that his job performance steadily declines to such an extent that he ends up working no more than one or two days a week, if that, for himself, because he "can't stand authority!" Needless to say, this means that the alcoholic is in serious trouble, and desperate measures may consequently be called for.

Should a family intervention then be done? Many women ask me that question.

The problem arises when a spouse is not yet ready to go through an intervention. To try and make a spouse opt for an intervention too early in her recovery is not a good idea. Let me say here that *most* interventions are successful: *when* the family is *ready* for them. Far better, in such circumstances, for the spouse of the alcoholic to be encouraged to wait until she is definitely ready to face the consequences of an intervention.

God has mercy on us in our weakness. Sometimes

we feel that we just can't carry through with anything, He just picks us up and carries us where we're supposed to be.

I have worked with several women who thought that they were strong enough to carry out an intervention. Right before the intervention was supposed to take place, they had to pull out. They felt very bad about this, but I told them it was okay. I could say this because actually all that they did was to put it on the shelf, so to speak. It just means that *at the moment* they can't follow through with an intervention. But if they think they can carry it through in the future, they'll know what they've been through, and they will be the stronger for it.

What's unfortunate is that often we have a situation where, on the one hand, there are some counselors who want to force the alcoholic to get sober no matter how sick the family is. They, understandably, identify with the alcoholic. What I suggest to counselors is to always be attuned to the deepest fears of the family. If you try to rush them, the families will drop out of counseling, and then there will be *no* chance for an intervention. On the other hand, we have people who are always very adamantly against intervention. They believe that intervention is just another way of making the family subordinate to the needs of the alcoholic. Obviously, if you have a situation in which an alcoholic has a job in a company that offers an Employee Assistance Program, that is often the perfect means by which to bypass this conflict.

Perhaps one of the things a spouse can do, if she wants to keep her name out of it, is to find out quietly if her husband's company has an Employee Assistance Program. She could call the personnel office and ask about it just as someone who is interested in that kind of information. That would not be an unusual call to make. If there is such a program at that company, the spouse could then call the coordinator of the program and talk to him or her.

If you *are* ready to *think* about an intervention, call your nearest private alcoholism treatment center (ask Alcoholics Anonymous where there is one), and talk to the director at the treatment center. You should find that an experienced interventionist will carry the ball and lead the intervention for you. Once it is done, you will be relieved and find that it wasn't horrible to go through. Pray your way through it. The best that usually happens is the alcoholic goes to treatment and then AA; the worst? It's usually that he agrees to try ninety AA meetings in ninety days.

"Love conquers all things; let us too surrender to love." (Virgil)

3. "If I just don't make waves, maybe then it'll give me breathing space. Maybe he'll just get better, somehow, without having to get sober. Maybe I can get away with not doing anything."

Suggested Activities:
1. Try to attend an AA-sponsored Gratitude Breakfast or Dinner. These are arranged as a means of thanking people who sometimes forced some of the AA members into sobriety. These meetings are real eye-openers. When a man truly gets sober, he drops his resentment and is humbly grateful for the people who made him save his life.
2. If you've "held still" for a while, and a period of calm in your household has been followed by everything going crazy again, remind yourself that his disease won't "hold still," that alcoholism is

progressive and fatal and that without his getting treatment—AA—the disease will just get worse.

3. The next time a small crisis comes up—the kind of crisis that would ordinarily make you feel vulnerable—act as if you don't feel vulnerable at all.

15

Trust Your Gut Feeling
in Working with Professionals

Trust God.
Trust Yourself.
Trust Your Gut Feeling.
Trust Al-Anon.

I worked with Betina, a woman in her late fifties whose husband was an alcoholic. She told me of her past experience with a psychiatrist who helped her with many of her problems but who, unfortunately, did not know much about alcoholism. He finally admitted this, but not until after a long, grief-filled time for her. When she was about to marry her fiancé, who even then was an alcoholic, her psychiatrist told her that she wasn't to go ahead with the wedding. He didn't understand the addictive nature of what was going on and that, regardless of what anyone said, she was going to plunge ahead and marry her fiancé anyway.

After she had been married for a year and a half, she went back to the psychiatrist and told him that her husband had been violent towards her and that she was not going to let him back in the house until he went into treatment.

This psychiatrist told her that she was being mean and cruel towards an alcoholic man who could not help himself, that there was no possibility that he could get well, and that eventually he would have to be committed. Nevertheless, he finally agreed to see them both.

The first time the psychiatrist saw Betina's husband, he advised him to drink just a little and then stop. Naturally he couldn't do that—he couldn't stop drinking at all. The next time Betina's husband came to see the psychiatrist, he was disgusted with him because of his inability to stop drinking. The psychiatrist told him that he would have to be committed and this scared him to death. He was so frightened that he took off and couldn't be found for three months.

Joanne, another client of mine, has a fifteen-year-old son who is an alcoholic. He was arrested for a series of petty crimes that he had committed while drunk. He went before a judge who knew nothing about alcoholism and who did not believe that it was a disease. He sent the boy to a reform institution. After many more efforts to get him into treatment, the boy finally wound up in a local private mental hospital.

Joanne had various dealings with the professional staff of that mental hospital, all of whom did not accept the fact that alcoholism is a disease. The staff kept urging Joanne to love her son more, to take care of him more. Luckily Joanne was in Al-Anon and understood the importance of *tough love* when dealing with an alcoholic. She knew that tender, loving care would kill her son. She told this to the staff, and they were shocked at her attitude. Nonetheless, she found the strength to continue what she was supposed to do. This turned out to be the best thing for her son in the long run. But it was very difficult for her to do, even with the support of Al-Anon. This was because she, naturally, held professional mental health workers in high esteem. She found it difficult to confront these people, and to hold to the belief that her self-help group knew more about alcoholism than a well-known psychiatrist and his assistant social worker.

One good result was that, after this staff found that her son improved after she did things her way, they became open to finding out some new concepts on how to deal with alcoholics in mental hospitals.

Getting back to Betina, her psychiatrist told her that her husband was a manic-depressive and that it would be necessary to get to the root of his problem before he was going to be able to stop drinking. When she told this to me, I replied that it was a lot of baloney. I told her that there were tens of thousands of people in mental hospitals across the country who were being treated for various schizophrenic and manic-depressive disorders when their real problem was *alcoholic* schizophrenia and *alcoholic* manic-depression. This means that the schizophrenia and the manic-depression are drug-induced. When the drug, alcohol, is withdrawn for at least six months, the symptoms of mental illness seem to leave or at least to diminish greatly; after the person is sober for at least a year, the symptoms almost entirely disappear. After two years of sobriety they do disappear, unless this alcoholic is a true psychotic. And the percentage of psychotics in the alcoholic population is no higher than in the general population.

The primary disease is alcoholism; and alcohol, the drug, brings on these other behavior disorders. *Psychiatric problems don't cause alcoholism. There are a lot of psychiatric patients who don't drink and there are a lot of very normal people who become alcoholics.* If one attends an open AA meeting in a middle-class neighborhood, you can hear over and over again many "drunkalogs" (a person's history of their drinking) and what they were like before they drank. You hear many people say, "I don't know why I became an alcoholic; I was a football star," or "I was a normal, regular kind of person," or "I married a wonderful woman, a beautiful lady. We had three gorgeous children, I had a great career, and I did nothing but drink socially. Why did I become an alcoholic? I really don't know." Then you find that very often this person had a parent who was an alcoholic, which means that he had a genetic predisposition towards becoming an alcoholic himself if he drank. Thus we come back to the disease concept of alcoholism. This means that the disease is *physiologically induced and that the mental problems come after the onset of alcoholism.*

My suggestion to people who are going to therapists who truly do not understand the truth about alcoholism is to provide them with books and pamphlets about this disease. It's true that reliable information about alcoholism is sadly lacking. Until a few years ago, in medical schools across the country, information about alcoholism was only taught to doctors for about thirty minutes. Alcoholism is the number one public health problem in the country, according to the American Medical Association, and it's only been within the last few years that some medical schools began teaching about how to deal with the alcoholic. But most doctors are still not learning how to deal with the *families* of alcoholics.

So if you have a doctor or a mental health professional who doesn't *seem* to know anything about alcoholism, you're probably right to assume that the person doesn't know much about alcoholism. Most mental health professionals learn only statistics about alcohol; they learn all the mechanics about alcoholic behavior and withdrawal, but they still have a mental-health approach to alcoholism. That approach affirms that if you get rid of the problems in an alcoholic's life—*then* you can get rid of the drinking. This is opposed to the disease-concept approach that points out that you must stop drinking *first* before you can effectively deal with the problems.

In this area I would say, trust your Higher Power, trust yourself, *trust the Al-Anon and the AA approach*. They work. *The mental-health approach —as opposed to the primary disease concept—does not work in alcoholism.* Nor does it get the families well. As a friend once told me, he spent thirty thousand dollars over fifteen years to get his wife sober and she's still going to her psychiatrist. The psychiatrist is still trying to find a way for her to deal with her underlying problems, after which *then* maybe she'll want to stop drinking. There's a good chance that this woman will die before the psychiatrist finds out the right way to help her.

"As soon as you trust yourself, you will know how to live." (Johann Wolfgang von Goethe)

Write On:

1. "I've had the following experiences in dealing with lawyers, social workers, judges, therapists, et al. concerning the alcoholism in our family." (Write about each situation specifically.)

2. "After each such experience I had the following feelings:"

3. "After reading the preceding chapter, I have the following feelings about trusting my own responses, and not feeling guilty and/or crazy with regard to what alcoholism has done to me and my family:"

Suggested Activities:

1. Before carrying out any activity, try to do it in the light of the following questions: Is this necessary? Is it honest? If you can answer affirmatively to these questions, try to follow through, if you can, with kindness. This will increase your effectiveness, build your dignity, add to your spiritual strength, and go a long way to prevent guilt.

2. You may want to contact the helping professionals you've had to deal with—or keep this in mind when you have dealings in the future with members of the helping professions—and help educate them about the disease of alcoholism for the sake of other alcoholic families.

16

The Alcoholic and the Kids vs. "Mean Mommy"

Many professionals think you're coming from a position of strength: *they don't see how the alcoholic is pulling your terror-strings.*

The kids see you the same way.

Following the Al-Anon program will bring healing to you, and will help your children see reality.

The kids are in the middle and they see you as a screaming person who's always yelling at poor, sick daddy. He vacillates between being a stumbling-down, acting-out alcoholic and being super-loving towards the kids. He shows up at their school during recess and brings them candy (even though he's not working); he buys them expensive gifts that the family can't afford and which you have to take back so that you'll be able to pay some of the bills. He does everything to prove that he's a nice guy and that you're the mean mommy.

It's bad enough to have to deal with this within the family, but it may even get worse if members of the helping professions are involved, as well. For instance, if at some time or another you, the non-alcoholic spouse, have to deal with members of the helping profession who are trying to be of assistance to your family, you may find that they don't understand, or are unsympathetic to, your situation. Sometimes when these people visit your household, what they see is *your* anger. They have no idea of what you've been through with your husband. They don't know that your husband can come off as totally (falsely) charming to the outside world. And they don't realize that this makes you—who knows what's *really* going on—feel at once absolutely crazy and absolutely enraged.

A recovering alcoholic told me what happened once with him and his first wife in California. He got her crazily angry by goading her and goading her, following her from room to room, and he kept it up for about six hours until she screamed at him, picked up something to hit him with and started to chase him. He immediately ran out of the house and she furiously chased after him through the back yard and into the neighborhood. Somebody saw what was going on and called the police. They came promptly while she was still brandishing the stick. At once her husband changed into a conciliatory professional man, confident in his field. He flashed his credentials (she, of course, had none). The police were very impressed with him and immediately concluded that his wife was the one who was totally crazy. As a result, she got so frustrated and angry at the way things were turning out that she hit a policeman on the arm, in frustration. She was promptly arrested and taken off to jail. Her husband let her stay there for the whole night to "teach her a lesson." Meanwhile he went home and got drunk.

The next morning he told her that he would arrange for her release, *provided that she had learned her lesson.* She didn't want to spend any *more* time in jail, so she had to agree. You can imagine what this situation did for her self-esteem.

This scene is very typical of families of alcoholics. People in the outside world—if they haven't lived with this—have no idea of the insanity that goes on in alcoholic families. On top of it all, this very same family is often referred to a therapist who is probably as unknowledgable as everyone else as to what goes on in alcoholic families. The alcoholic can successfully play his calm, reasonable role with the therapist. He will walk into the therapist's office all reasonable, detached, and very ready to "work well" with him. The wife, on the other hand, may stamp in like a maniac, furious and raging, because she knows what's going on and realizes that she has very little chance to have her side of the story given a fair hearing. Who's going to believe her? Appearances are against her. It's too easy to believe that what the alcoholic says is true—that *she's* the crazy one.

The therapist will tell her that her rage is inappropriate and that her husband is a reasonable man. The wife will respond with her account of what the alcoholic has been doing and how he's been acting, and the therapist will look at her as if she's crazy. At the very least, he'll think she's exaggerating.

The outside world confirms to the non-alcoholic spouse that she's crazy. It plays the same game *with* the alcoholic that he plays at home—"You and me versus 'mean mommy.' " That makes it easier for him to continue with the same game at home. Look at all the support he's getting. How can he lose?

What can the spouse do about this? The most important thing to do is to go to Al-Anon meetings on a regular basis. Specifically, go with the intention of rapidly becoming a participant and not just a spectator. And don't give up. If you don't like one Al-Anon group, seek out another one and keep looking until you can find one or more that you are comfortable with. Get the names and phone numbers of other people who attend these meetings. Call them up when things are rough. Get a sponsor. Listen to the stories of other people. Realize that you're not alone and that you are not unique. That is one of the best defenses against accusations of insanity.

If you start to understand that this particular kind of craziness is *alcoholic,* it will become a bigger and bigger buffer against the craziness you encounter in living with your alcoholic spouse. As a result, you will find that you will not have to react so strongly when the same kind of thing happens again. After a while you will not have to react at all against it. Instead, after a while, you'll learn to respond in a sane, adult way. And when you calm down—and you will be able to do so—you'll find yourself capable of responding in an appropriate manner. The alcoholic, not you, will be the one who blows up.

You see, he's only staying calm because you're the one who is blowing up. When he can't elicit the kind of response from you that he really wants any more, he's the one who will start reacting crazily—and more publicly. Then people will start seeing his alcoholism, and the problems it's been causing, for what it really is. And when other people, outside of the family, start telling the alcoholic that he has a problem, he then has a greater chance of waking up and accepting his own problem as his own, and then doing what must be done to get sober.

If you're blowing up and reacting to his alcoholism (which is what is really going on) he'll think he is being victorious and that his alcoholism is putting him on the winning side. It's crazy, but that's how he thinks. He thinks he is doing well if he's getting you to react and look crazy.

Underneath it all, of course, the guilt is building up in him. He knows what he's really doing. You don't even have to say it. That guilt is helping him to continue drinking.

I know that this is difficult to believe but it's absolutely true. By and large, alcoholics are not psychopaths. The overwhelming majority of alcoholics do have a conscience, even though they seem not to. They *act as if* they don't have consciences. But still the truth is exactly the opposite. When they get sober, the overwhelming majority are really very moral people.

Now, as far as your children go, it'll take them awhile to change their attitudes from seeing you as "mean mommy." They'll be confused for a while, but they're going to start seeing the reality. When they start seeing that you've become relatively calm, you're going to be an example to them and they, as a result, will become much more willing to get help. It's going to take time, but for you to feel good about yourself the investment of time and energy is worth it. That hour a day at Al-Anon a few times a week is going to make all the difference in the world. It will give you back your peace of mind.

"The peace of God which passeth all understanding, shall keep your hearts and minds." (Phil. 4:7)

Write On:

How you and your alcoholic spouse possibly appear to each of your children. This will put objective light on the problem and allow you to do something about it more effectively.

Suggested Activity:

If a bill collector bothers you about a bill that is entirely the alcoholic's responsibility, you may want to quietly inform that collector of the fact. You may also want to let him know how to contact the person responsible for the bill. It will help calm you down and it will increase the pain of the consequences of the alcoholic's drinking. (This is very important for him.) It will also help straighten out the family roles, thereby letting your children see reality more clearly.

17

Praying for People
You Justifiably Resent

You don't have to like someone to pray for them so that you get well.
Prayer is therapeutic.

Probably heading up the list of people to pray for, whom you justifiably resent, is the alcoholic with whom you're involved. Probably the resentment is not just based on the present, but also on the future. In other words, it's easy enough to resent him for what he's doing this very day.

But a lot of the rage is projection. You fear that he will stay rotten, and that you will have to live with this for the rest of your life. It feels like a jail sentence.

This is, for the most part, based on a false assumption. Even if he stays the same as he is now, you're going to go to Al-Anon or counseling; you're going to do what needs to be done to get yourself well. Therefore, regardless of what he does or continues to be, you're not going to be the same person six months or a year from now; you're going to be very different. That means that your needs, and especially your wants, are going to change. Your ways of dealing with all of his junk are going to change. You're going to get so well that you will not want to put up with it and you won't feel like you need to.

When you get well you're not going to feel as if you *have* to put up with all that junk. Then you're going to be free. You're going to feel free to make decisions not to live with that junk, whatever that word means to you, whatever form it takes in your marriage.

God does not want you to live in junk. He does not want you to live with fear, indecision, uncertainty and despair. He wants you to live joyfully in joyful situations. And God wants you to be able to free yourself from unacceptable situations. If it means at this moment that you escape a painful situation by going into another room or out of the house altogether, He wants you to feel free to do that. That's what I believe God wants for me and I believe God wants that for all of His children. I don't believe that He wants us to suffer. I think that's a sick concept, part of the alcoholic family sickness, the feeling that God's getting ready to punish us at any minute. Getting well is feeling God's love and knowing that He wants our healing.

So, if getting well sets us free to make choices, part of the getting-well process is to begin to throw off the feelings about the alcoholic that really come from his disease. We get rid of them so we can be free of their burden, so we don't have to carry them around any more. One of the ways we carry his disease around on us is to carry that resentment about his sick alcoholic behavior. The way to get rid of that is to pray for him. If you have to say in your prayer, "God, I don't mean this. I don't like him, I can't stand him, but please give him health, wealth and happiness," do it that way. Be honest with God. Tell Him how you feel. But pray for the alcoholic. Eventually, if you pray for him daily, wishing for him what you would wish for yourself, it will heal you of resentment. And after you pray for him you can drop it for the rest of the day and go on and live *your* life.

"Only the brave know how to forgive." (Laurence Sterne)

Write On:

Specific instances when you engaged in cata-strophic expectations, and were sure that things were going to be terrible, but which turned out either just fine or very different from what you expected.

Suggested Activity:

Tell yourself that God doesn't want you to live in fear, uncertainty and despair. Tell yourself also that when you feel like these conditions are coming upon you inevitably, it is your disease talking and nothing else.

18

Dealing with Irrational Guilt

Having fun is healing.
Only God is expected to be perfect.

Probably the two most important factors holding back a spouse of an alcoholic from making gains in her spiritual growth are fear of losing the alcoholic and guilt. Several types of fear are involved: fears that he'll die, that he'll leave her, that he'll humiliate her, that financial problems will cause a split, and so forth. But most of the guilt is probably irrational.

I'd like to talk about a special kind of guilt that I see in the alcoholic household. Many spouses of alcoholics are themselves the adult children of alcoholics. Often they do not even recognize that their parents were alcoholics. They only want to remember the good about their parents. Very often, just *because* they come from alcoholic families, the spouses of alcoholics are guilt-ridden. They are also perfectionists. They have a spiritual meticulousness which will not enable them to get rid of the guilt, and can also be part and parcel of their spiritual sickness.

Most clients who come to see me talk very much in depth about their character defects. I don't have to encourage a spouse of an alcoholic to do so. It's what she focuses on immediately. She concentrates on every tiny little thing she's doing wrong; very often, if she can't find anything else that she's done wrong, she'll still keep looking.

Sometimes in the spouse of an alcoholic, her spiritual sickness is disguised as a virtue. My own mother, who lived with an alcoholic husband, was called "clean-crazy" by her whole family. She paid an enormous amount of attention to the details of house-cleaning, but felt powerless about everything else that was going on. She could not face the real problems at all; she just lived with them for twenty-eight years.

Meticulousness, perfectionism, is part and parcel of the family disease; it will do nothing to further your spiritual growth.

The spouse of the alcoholic often tries to be absolutely perfect in every area *so that she has the right to be able to do what she has to do to get well.*

If you practice having fun daily, much of that perfectionism will melt, and you will progress in healing much faster.

"There is no fear in love; but perfect love casteth out fear." (1 John 4:18)

Facts:

1. All spouses of alcoholics have irrational guilt.

2. All adult children of alcoholics who marry alcoholics have *double* doses of irrational guilt.

Write On:

Keep a record today of all the times you have thoughts that do no good to your feelings of self-esteem and self-worth.

Suggested Activity:

See if this record you kept doesn't start to seem tiresome. If it does, it shows that you have made a major step toward abandoning thoughts that do you no good. (If it's not tiresome, keep that record for a solid week. After that, you may start to tire of all that junk.)

19

Saying Alcoholism Is a Disease Goes Deeper Than We Think

AA enables an alcoholic not only to stay sober, but to recover mentally and spiritually.

Attend some open-to-the-public AA meetings, as well as going to Al-Anon regularly.

If he gets sober and goes to AA on a daily basis, he will get better despite himself.

It's one thing to say that alcoholism is a disease and another thing to really believe it. With most recovering alcoholics, it takes years before they fully accept the deeper implications of what it means to say they have a disease. If it takes an alcoholic a long time to realize this, you can be sure that it's going to take the spouse a long time too.

What does it mean to say that alcoholism is a disease? It's a mental, physical and spiritual disease, but it starts off physically. There are many people who go through life drinking heavily and never become alcoholics. Other people have a physiological predisposition to alcoholism; if they drink enough, or even start drinking, at any age, they will become instant alcoholics.

An example of this: I know a woman who is a recovering alcoholic. She was given alcohol to drink when she was just a baby and she immediately became addicted. This person was not a "sinful" baby; she had a predisposition to alcohol because she had two addicted parents. It was virtually inevitable that, if she drank, she would become an alcoholic.

If you don't want to believe that alcoholism starts off as a physical illness and that the intake of alcohol causes all those other mental and spiritual problems, then look at the multitudes of people in Alcoholics Anonymous. They did not really have any more than the general population's average amount of mental or spiritual problems before they became alcoholics. Many were just leading rather normal lives. But their social drinking turned into alcoholism and that "line was crossed over." And, when they stopped drinking, they went back to being regular people.

Now sometimes, if one is understandably angry at an alcoholic, it's possible to say to yourself, "Oh, even *recovering* alcoholics are crazy, sick people." But is that the truth? Perhaps we don't hear about the average recovering alcoholic because he's not, so to speak, standing up and waving a banner. He's just going about his business and doing what he's supposed to do.

I think that if you read the literature on alcoholism, you will be better able to understand that this is a disease. When you know it's a disease and you know what the disease is all about, you'll be able to have a lot more hope. Then you know that even though he acts terribly, he has a good chance to clear up in his mind, soul and heart if he goes to AA on a regular basis, puts down that booze and stays sober.

"What doth the Lord require of thee, but to do justly, and to love mercy, and to walk humbly with thy God." (Mic. 6:8)

Write On:

"He's been an alcoholic for *so* long. How would he ever know how to act decently again, even if he stopped drinking?"

Suggested Activity:

Attend some "open" meetings (where non-alcoholics are welcome) of Alcoholics Anonymous and listen to some of the members' stories of recovery.

20
You're Not Trapped

No situation is forever.
Change is a part of living.
Start expecting good things to happen to you.

We all know the symptoms of chronic, low-level depression. We let our hair get all ratty, we don't go to the dentist when we should, we keep gaining weight, or losing it, when we're not supposed to, and so forth. Things just seem to be falling apart. We can't get it together and we don't necessarily feel like doing anything. And that's part of what it's like when you feel that you're trapped.

A woman I know, who was in the last stages of her marriage to an alcoholic, was in a deep, unremitting depression. She couldn't free herself from this depression no matter what anybody said. Everything seemed hopeless. Finally her sister took her out to dinner at a nice restaurant that this woman was too depressed to appreciate. She just sat there and mechanically ate, scarcely paying attention to anything. But during dinner her sister kept telling her, "You are not trapped; you are not trapped." The words finally sank in and they gave her hope. She realized that she was not in fact trapped, that she didn't have to live in terrible situations forever. That dinner marked the beginning of her recovery.

One of the traits of the alcoholic is intensity; it's always all or nothing. The alcoholic often says to himself that the pain he is feeling right now is unbearable, that he can't stand it, that it will last forever and never go away. The reason that the literature about alcoholism calls family members co-alcoholics is because these family members very often exhibit the same patterns of behavior as the alcoholic, with the exception of the drinking problem. Thus, this same intensity is characteristic of members of the alcoholic's family too. This has a great deal to do with their feelings of being hopelessly trapped. They too think that the situation is unbearable and will last forever.

A person who does not, and has never, lived with alcoholism very often has a more balanced view of life. He might realize that the problem of living in a particular situation is difficult, but he does not magnify the problem out of all proportion to its actual seriousness. What does help is to realize that there are options available and to step back and take an inventory of your total life situation, to put the alcoholism in its place.

Sometimes the way to get to that point is through a

side door, so to speak. Many times that side door is gratitude. By that I mean that when one is grateful for what is good in one's life, one begins to calm down. When you feel overwhelmed, you feel like you have to deal with everything all the time and it rapidly gets to be too much. But realizing that there are major things that are already okay in your life is necessary too.

Another way to avoid feeling trapped is to get back to living one day at a time. Again, I don't mean this as a way to trick you into thinking that living with this junk the rest of your life is okay if only you'll take it one day at a time. What I'm saying is: okay, you're in this rotten situation today. But think back on how many times in your life something has changed overnight. Anything can happen. The possibilities are limitless.

One of the major factors in feeling trapped is thinking erroneously. Whether we like it or not, everything is always changing. So it is incorrect to think that a certain bad situation is going to be the same for the rest of your life. That is just not true. All sorts of others things are going to happen. What you deal with tomorrow can be a whole different ball of wax from what you have to deal with today. Each day is fraught with possibilities that are constantly changing. To make yourself think that you'll have to deal with a particular bad situation for the rest of your life is simply unreal.

Another problem is that the alcoholic and his

family have a tendency to anticipate a future full of doom. They feel that things will never get better. That's why in the AA program they tell the alcoholic that, as he gets better and more sober, he will gradually lose his feeling of "impending doom." If you go into treatment, you will start to drop that feeling of impending doom.

Usually, if the family looks into the future, they may anticipate that the alcoholic, after treatment, will be in terrific shape for a short while. But then they will gloomily predict. "Oh, yeah. But then it's all going to fall apart again." If this is the case with you, you must tell yourself that you think this way not because you are a negative person or because it is the truth, but because that way of thinking is part and parcel of the alcoholic family illness. To realize this helps a lot towards changing one's attitudes about the future and what it holds.

If you want to think about the future, *expect good*. That's what they say in AA and I think it is terrific.

Of course that does not mean that everything will always be peachy keen with the alcoholic. It *does* mean that all kinds of twists of events and changes in circumstances can bring good to you so that you will be stronger, calmer and healthier. *And if you keep going to Al-Anon, to treatment, you're going to get well despite yourself.*

"Thou art a God ready to pardon, gracious and merciful, slow to anger and of great kindness." (Neh. 9:17)

Suggested Activity:

To gain a clearer perspective on your life situation, try, when talking about it, to use words that are less emotionally laden. Use, for example, a word like "difficult" instead of "horrible." Think about the future in terms of possibilities, not problems.

21

From Rage to Pity: a Trap

You are not the vulnerable one.
Give yourself permission to have fun.

Marge was telling me how she had come a long way in Al-Anon and counseling. To a large degree she had learned to detach, especially in situations in which her husband tried to "get to her."

This is what typically happened. They would be out in some kind of social situation, and suddenly he would notice another woman. He would turn to his wife and give her "that look," that kind of puffed-up look that so enraged her. She knew he couldn't possibly be genuinely interested in the woman he had noticed, but still he would give her that look with the raised eyebrows and a sort of big-eyed stare, as if to say, "Aha, I can squelch you. See how I'm looking at her?"

There was no way his wife could effectively protest. She would accuse him of "doing it again," after which he would hotly deny doing anything and tell her that she was crazy. Then they would get into a big argument.

It took a long time before Marge learned how to deal effectively with this kind of a problem. But after a time, she learned how to turn the tables on him.

When they were out in public together and walking down the street, she would keep an eye out for attractive men. When she spotted one, she would give him a long, appreciative look, realizing that her husband was very aware of what she was doing. She was not at all genuinely attracted to these men, but she was out to prove to her husband that two could play his game. It served to make her feel much less helpless.

This worked for a few months until she started feeling really guilty about doing it. Then she finally stopped because it wasn't worth the guilt. But at least it also helped her to go one further step up in not feeling so helpless in her relationship with her alcoholic husband.

The next thing she found that she was able to do was to just ignore him when he got into his junk. She was not able to do this all the time, but she did manage it fairly frequently. She would express slight annoyance, but she could look at him as if he were just plain crazy.

The next step she found herself able to take was to ignore him totally, pretend to herself that it just wasn't happening, and smile. And she then saw something she had never seen before. She saw that when she smiled, he would smile back in some confusion. A little while later, she would notice that he was looking slightly depressed. She soon realized what it was all about. He had been trying to make himself feel good at her expense. He did what he did to get himself out of his chronic depression, to puff himself up. When that didn't work, he went further down into his depression. Then she knew that she had given his problem back to him, and that he would have to deal with that depression and himself. She then, for the first time, realized that he really hadn't been attracted to any of those other women at all. He had just been using them to play a game with her.

Then she got to a new stage. She started realizing that when she was not at her very best emotionally, she would slip back into reacting and being vulnerable. Then he would go back to his old tricks again. She became inwardly enraged and depressed at the idea that she would always have to stay on her toes and keep her defense up so that he wouldn't "do it."

She started to have very gloomy thoughts about the future. She thought, "My God, suppose in a couple of years I get real sick and I'm vulnerable and he starts doing this junk over and over again. How will I deal with it when I'm down? Why do I have to go through all of this anyway?" She was enraged by this. Sometimes her rage took the form of held-in depression. She realized that she was, so to speak, sleeping with one eye open. And then a lot of times her husband would become super-sweet or do something that would just make her feel overwhelming love or pity towards him. She started realizing that she was running back and forth in her mind from rage to pity and back again. And she didn't know what to do about it.

I suggested to Marge that she look at this situation in several ways. First of all, she should slightly lower her expectations of herself. I believed that her expectation of herself was that she get rid of her husband, immediately get well herself, find somebody who was terrific and live happily ever after. I had to tell her that things don't often happen that way. I told her that if she left her marriage, or if her alcoholic husband walked out on her and never came back, she'd still be left with being the way she is, with all those behavior patterns unconsciously ingrained— really deeply. Therefore, there was a good chance that she would be one of the 75 percent of ex-wives of alcoholics who marry another alcoholic or another "crazy" or needy man.

I explained that there are ways to detach oneself from painful situations that one cannot, yet, physically leave, and one of these is to see the situation as a *training ground* for her to get well. I also said that when she really gets well and strong within herself, when she learns to be dependent on her Higher Power and not on her husband, she'll be able to deal wisely and calmly with everything that happens to her in her life. But right now she had an opportunity to grow and get strong. I told her that if she was still at a point where she felt she had to sleep with one eye open, so to speak, and where she was still very vulnerable to her alcoholic husband, that was very understandable. But when she really gets well, what he says will not matter very much. Granted, it would probably be annoying—the drinking alcoholic is a past-master at "getting at the jugular"—but she still would be able to feel that she had a choice about how to deal with the situation. It would even be okay if she decided that she had to physically get away from the situation.

"Meanwhile," I said, "if you don't feel strong enough to leave that situation or to make him leave, even temporarily, then you have to look at the situation in another way. Alcoholism, after all, is a disease of attitudes.

"It might help to realize and understand that you are making the alcoholic too important and yourself too unimportant. Actually, no matter what you think, he's a lot more dependent on you than you are on him. That's the reality of it. *The fact is, alcoholics don't hook up with weak women. You're really not as dependent on the situation as you think you are. That's just one of the illusions of alcoholism.*

"Try to see this period of time as a training ground to get well. And instead of letting your looks go, you can tell yourself that no matter what happens, you want to look and feel your best so that you can live longer and happier. As a person who had been in AA a long time said, 'If I would have known I would live so long and could have been so happy, I would have taken better care of myself.'

"One of the things that it is also good to remember is that as you get better, as your self-esteem grows, you will find that a lot of the guilt is eroded, leaving you free to make decisions. You'll be free to say that you're a child of God and know that you really mean it. You should say that to yourself right now, regularly, but the words will have more meaning to you as time goes on.

"God accepts you as you are. If you don't feel capable right now of making any kind of a choice, that's fine. You didn't get sick overnight, so it's unreasonable to expect that you'll get well overnight. It's important to slow down and remember that you can't have everything at once. To want too much right away can very quickly lead to depression. In fact, that's part of the alcoholic family illness; it's your disease talking when you feel that way. Remembering that will help to keep everything in perspective.

"It's also important to give yourself credit for small victories. If you think you're too dependent on your alcoholic husband, try to find ways to cut down on that dependence. Call him at work less often, for example. Try to concentrate on doing what a normal, healthy wife does during the course of a normal day. It's hard at first, but it will get easier. Get the body there and the mind will follow."

"Self-reliance, the height and perfection of man, is reliance on God." (Ralph Waldo Emerson)

Write On:

The many ways through which the alcoholic has convinced you that you are the vulnerable one. Then list your strengths.

Suggested Activities:

1. Make a list of all the things you were going to do today.

2. Prioritize that list; postpone half of them.

3. Do one-half of what is left on the list.

4. Forget the rest of the list and spend the rest of the day joyfully lazing around.

22

Getting Help

The problem can't get better by itself.
Alcoholism is a progressive disease.
AA and Al-Anon are there to help.

A spouse of an alcoholic will often say that she has
been to get help. She will point out that she's been to
a therapist or a counselor, and that both she and her
husband have gone together to a marriage counselor.
But how much good does it do?

Unfortunately (though hopefully it's starting to
change in this country), most helping professionals
simply do not understand alcoholism. When the
spouse goes to a counselor, the counselor tells the
spouse about her inappropriate rage. If the spouse
goes to a clergyman, the clergyman will say that the
spouse should be loving her alcoholic husband more.
Or she goes to counseling for many months and the
counselor does nothing but talk about her childhood
and her relationship with her parents; there is
scarcely any talk at all about alcoholism. Finally—

and very understandably—the spouse will just leave therapy, feeling that no one has ever really gotten to the heart of the issue.

Another possible outcome is this: The spouse might tell her husband that now she knows that he is an alcoholic and that the only alternative for her is to go to Al-Anon in order to learn how to cope with it. Her husband will panic, for some reason, and tell her not to go, that he'll control his drinking. The spouse accepts what she hopes will be a long-term trade-off, and everything is okay for a while. He does control his drinking for a short period, and this fact is very confusing to her. After all, how can he be able to control his drinking and still be an alcoholic? She gets the idea that he is basically okay, even when he goes back again to drinking heavily. He, feeling very much in power, may tell her at this point that the reason she thought he was an alcoholic was because one of her relatives had a drinking problem, and she "sees it everywhere," that nothing is really wrong, that he doesn't get drunk every day, and besides, all the guys in the office "tie one on" every afternoon after work. He may seriously try to convince her that she is the one with the problem and not him. Even though she knows better, and she has submerged the rage and is depressed, he has her believing that she is crazy.

The fact is, just because someone doesn't drink every day does not mean that he's not an alcoholic. You hear the same story every day in AA from recovering alcoholics. They will say that they were binge drinkers. They'd drink only on weekends, or only Mondays through Wednesdays, or even only once a month. But they were still alcoholics. It's often only at the very late, deteriorative stages of alcoholism that alcoholics have to resort to daily, around-the-clock maintenance drinking.

Another issue that confuses the spouse is that the alcoholic can control his drinking *sometimes*. He doesn't get drunk all of the time. He doesn't always lose control. This is true of many middle-stage alcoholics. Total loss of control often does not occur until the later stages of alcoholism.

Another myth is represented in the words, "Well, he's sober sometimes."

When a counselee tells me that, I have to ask, "How often is he sober?"

The response is usually something like, "Well, he's usually sober Mondays through Thursdays." *But that's not sober*. It takes thirty days for the alcohol to get out of a person's system, and it takes much longer for an individual to go through the protracted withdrawal syndrome and get really sober. Even to get slightly dry, the same thirty-day, alcohol-free period is required. And that means going without one single drink.

Another myth associated with alcoholism often stops a woman from getting help herself. That myth says that the situation will get better all by itself. What she is not aware of is the progressive nature of the disease. Even if the alcoholic controls his drinking for an extended period of time—usually to try to prove to people that he's not an alcoholic—he can't hold on forever. Sooner or later he'll get roaring drunk. But in the meantime, his spouse may be deceived into thinking that he's actually getting better.

But it *can't* get better. Once you have the disease of alcoholism, that's it. There's no turning back. The disease is progressive and fatal.

A lot of people try to fool themselves about this. Sometimes a woman will say to me, "Well, my husband isn't as bad as my father was. My father was really in bad shape, and my husband isn't nearly as bad as that." I have to respond by saying that it isn't as if there are different types of alcoholism. It's all one disease. It's a disease which is on a continuum and is progressive for everyone who has it. That woman's father might have been thrown into a late stage of alcoholism rather quickly in his life, while her husband may be one of those—and there are a lot of them—who limp along for a considerable time at an earlier stage of the disease before proceeding—and it's inevitable—to a later stage. But one never knows the time table with each individual.

Even if an alcoholic stops drinking, his disease still continues to progress. That's a very unfortunate, insidious thing about alcoholism which few people, unless they are recovering alcoholics in AA, know about. You hear in AA about people who are sober for a long period and who then go out to drink because they think that they can "handle it." What happens? Within a few months, often, they're dead, unless they are fortunate enough to get back to AA. That's why the alcoholic has to continue to go to AA for treatment, to remind himself that he has a disease that won't go away.

Another factor to understand is that if your husband is taking any kind of drug or tranquilizer, and drinking at the same time, the drugs will have a deadly multiplier effect. Even if he doesn't die, the multiplier effect will throw him into a later stage of alcoholism. Nor does it matter if the substance of the pill is supposedly non-addictive; if he's an alcoholic, many substances that are non-addictive to non-alcoholics are addictive for him.

It's important to realize that your wanting to get help is often hindered by his convincing you that he doesn't have the disease of alcoholism. The more that you can learn about this disease, the more you can crack through this denial and get the help you need.

"Yea, though I walk through the valley of the shadow of death, I will fear no evil: for thou art with me; thy rod and thy staff they comfort me." (Ps. 23:4)

Write On:
The myths that stop you from getting help.

Suggested Activity:
If your spouse gets angry when you attend Al-Anon, tell yourself that it's his disease, not him, that is doing the talking. That disease wants him to die from alcoholism; it also wants you to go crazy and your kids to marry and/or become alcoholics.

23

If You and the Alcoholic
Are Separated and You Cannot
Stop Being Afraid or Angry

Your feelings are normal human emotions.
You cannot love everyone in the world.
Some people may not like you, but that's their business.

Joyce told me that during her divorce trial her alcoholic husband pulled her strings again to make her feel guilty. She didn't know exactly how it happened, she just knew that it happened. So I asked her to go back and go through the steps of what happened at that trial.

It turned out that he had done the one thing that would not make her feel angry, but pity for him. He walked up to her and cried and told her that he was so sorry for everything that he had done. What was the result? She felt deeply sorry for this guy who was sitting there crying. Then his attorney asked her and her attorney if she would allow him to keep the trailer, which was joint property, but he had been living in.

They had a small house and a large trailer. Because she had custody of the children, she kept the house and raised the children there. He was to have sold the trailer, split the money with her, and, in addition, given her alimony. What it boiled down to was that Joyce felt very guilty about following through, insisting that the trailer be sold, and then insisting on her share of the money. Instead of doing this, she agreed that he could stay in the trailer, and asked only that he continue to send her a small amount of money every month.

So the contract was drawn up to the effect that if he continued to send her money, the trailer would not have to be sold. She told her lawyer that one of her husband's problems was that he had a lot of resentment about paying anybody anything, and that he probably would not pay her regularly. Her lawyer advised to give him a chance, even though he saw that her husband had been dragging his feet throughout all of the divorce proceedings, and had done a lot towards making her feel guilty, and a lot towards preventing her from getting what was due to her.

She let this drag on for six months. She received not a penny. One day she and her lawyer were speaking about the issue and he said, "We're just going to have to get that trailer sold, get your half of the money and let that be that. We just can't allow him any more time."

When Joyce talked to me about this afterwards she was not feeling terrific. She felt very depressed and angry about the fact that she was having to spend lawyers' fees to get this money, whereas if she had stuck to her guns in the first place, the matter would have long since been settled. On the other hand, she was feeling guilty about depriving her ex-husband of a place to live. I reminded her about her relationship with her husband and what it had *really* been like. I reminded her about all the times when she had come to me and told me how he had goaded her and goaded her into a situation that was untenable; then, when she blew up and did what she had to do, she felt so guilty. He made the guilt worse by crying and feeling remorseful and then she pitied him. Then, in the very next minute, he would be at it again—which, if nothing else, proved that his remorse was really nothing more than a facade, nothing more than part of the total, sick manipulation of the disease. I told her that if she could just realize that she was saying "no" to his disease rather than to him, that she was not going to allow this disease to disrupt her life any more, then she would be taking a giant step toward getting well.

When she had to do this and took a few other actions in the same manner, she found that it became easier each time she did them. She soon realized that God was not going to punish her. When she went to Al-Anon meetings and heard stories very similar to her own, she could calm down. I also reminded her—

as regards the problem with the trailer—that she was just following through on a business transaction like a regular person. Her ex-husband simply had to face up to the facts. He knew that if he didn't make the payments he would be in danger of losing the trailer. And now he was going to lose it. It was as simple as that.

Joyce told me that she was also fearful of what his friends would think. I told her that what his friends thought would depend on where they were coming from. His drinking alcoholic friends would probably say that she was terrible and giving him a bad deal, etc. If he had some friends and co-workers who understood the real nature of the family disease of alcoholism, they would probably look at the situation logically and realize that an agreement had probably been made and that, if he was forced to sell the trailer, he had probably not been keeping up with the legally required payments. I also told her that she could not base her life on whether or not a few people were going to criticize her or not. As a well-known psychologist once said, "There are going to be about 50 percent of the people in the world who will like what you do; the other 50 percent are not going to approve of what you do." He went on to say that whenever he encountered anyone who disapproved of what he was doing, he would say, "Okay. Things are as they should be. This is one of those 50 percent."

Write On:

Let's say that you are separated from your alcoholic spouse. Your life is going along peacefully for a while, and suddenly he disrupts it in some way. Try to see it as an annoyance you just have to deal with, instead of as a catastrophe, and just get on with your life. You fall into his disease's trap when you let it have more importance than it should. (It helps, sometimes, to pretend that such situations are business situations and that you are dealing with a difficult customer or business rival. Write out a memo to yourself (as if to a supervisor), about how you are going to deal with the situation, and then go on with business as usual—living your life the way you want to live it.)

Suggested Activity:

Watch an entire television news program (international, national and local news) and think about how none of the people who appear on these programs know about the spouse you're separated from, how unimportant his activities are in relation to the rest of the world, and how none of thse people is judging you at all.

24

Will Counseling Help
a Drinking Alcoholic?

You cannot cause alcoholism.
You cannot cure alcoholism.
You cannot control alcoholism.

The success of counseling is 90 percent dependent on the honesty of the counselee. Since a drinking alcoholic, because of the nature of his disease, does not often tell the truth, the outcome of counseling is usually not favorable, to say the least, and often is disastrous.

To say that most drinking alcoholics don't tell the truth is part of the sad facts about alcoholism. Alcohol, the drug, acts upon the brain and the nervous system in such a way as to hold back the knowledge that he has a disease from the alcoholic. Everything that the drug alcohol does upon the body and the brain is self-protective to the disease, to guarantee that it stays there so that the alcoholic cannot really receive help. Because of the nature of his disease, he cannot, absolutely cannot, tell the truth about his alcoholism to a counselor, *unless he has surrendered*—and very few alcoholics have surrendered when they go to counseling.

Now, what is the difference between going to counseling and going to an alcoholism treatment center? At an alcoholism treatment center, the alcoholic will usually encounter trained-in-alcoholism counselors who are skilled in cracking through the denial of the alcoholic. They are *used* to the alcoholic not telling the truth about his drinking. They don't take it for granted that he's telling the truth when he says he only drinks a couple of drinks a night. They also do not believe that his problems are causing his alcoholism. They know that his alcoholism is causing his problems, and that he can't do anything at all about his problem until he stops drinking.

If your husband says he wants to go to counseling and you suggest an alcoholism treatment center, and AA, he may seem to have a lot of what appear to be reasonable objections to going. He may be an executive and express fears of losing his job if his boss finds out that he's going to AA. Well, that's a lot of baloney. If his alcoholism is so apparent even to him, I can guarantee that his co-workers and his employer know full well that he's an alcoholic. They would just be *relieved* to see him in a treatment center.

Very often the spouse swallows that denial because

she *too* denies. So often the alcoholic is virtually lying out in the street and his wife pulls him in and then does everything possible to prevent the neighbors from finding out. But they already know. They can hear the fights, they see the erratic driving and the stumbling footsteps. They see the red, puffy face and the beer belly (which is really a diseased and swollen liver). *The alcoholic and his family are fooling no one.*

Another thing the alcoholic who wants to get out of going for help says is that he'll get fired if it's learned that he's going for treatment. Alcoholism has, especially within the past few years, become recognized as a disease. Much of government and industry employers in all economic sectors are very glad to send a long-term employee to treatment. They don't want to lose that employee to alcoholism. They've invested too much in him. They'd be very glad to send him to treatment, knowing that in thirty days he'll come back a different kind of person and be able to perform decently on the job again.

Another problem that comes up is the question of marriage counseling. One of three things usually happens: The wife and the alcoholic go to marriage counseling. If the marriage counselor knows nothing about alcoholism, very often the wife will get disgusted and drop out of counseling. The husband will continue to go to this counselor, and thus further boost his denial of his problem with alcohol. He can come home, do what he wants, run around, do this, do that, *keep drinking,* and still legitimately claim that he's "in treatment" and everything's fine.

On the other hand, the alcoholic husband may drop counseling because the counselor focuses too closely on his drinking problem. But very often the counselor does not know enough about alcoholism and therefore does not know what to say to the alcoholic's wife about the problem. As a result, the wife becomes once again depressed and despairing.

If the counselor knows what he or she is doing, then an intervention may be set up; the alcoholic can be forced to go into treatment. Unfortunately, if this is performed by a person unskilled in alcoholic intervention, the results could be less than favorable. If you're interested in setting up an intervention, I suggest that you read the chapter on intervention in this book and then go see a counselor from an AA-oriented, private, alcoholism treatment center.

I would also check out the alcoholism treatment center that your husband agrees to go to to see if it too is AA-oriented. Unfortunately, some of them are not. Of course, any kind of treatment center is better than no treatment at all. But for the most part those that are not AA-oriented are mental-health oriented, which means they will ignore his drinking in favor of trying to get to the heart of some of his personal problems. The implicit idea is that once you solve your personal problems, your drinking will then automatically stop. But that's just not the way it is; it's the other way around. Once the alcoholic stops drinking, *then* he has a chance of solving his problems. But he has to stop drinking first.

If you're going to get involved in trying to find a good treatment center for your alcoholic, I think it's very important for you to work very hard at detaching yourself from the outcome of this endeavor. You should not get involved if you genuinely feel it is impossible for you to detach yourself. Let *him* be the problem-solver. *You* can give him this chapter to read. If he really wants to get well, then he will follow up on all these suggestions.

If he *doesn't* want to get well, nothing you say or do will make the slightest bit of difference. But if you feel that you *have* to give it your last, best shot, by all means then try and get him into a treatment center. But please understand that he may not follow through. *It's not the end of the world if he doesn't*. Someone else or something else may get him to follow through at some other time.

Once you've done everything you can, it's time for you to get back to your own life. Most important, of course, is to continue to go to Al-Anon. But whatever you do, it's important not to beat yourself on the head about the situation. Remember the three Cs: You cannot *cause* alcoholism, you cannot *cure* alcoholism and you cannot *control* alcoholism. The bottom line is, if you've done the best you can to get

Write On:

Specific times when you've tried, unsuccessfully, to persuade the alcoholic to get help, and how, afterwards, you felt, if you were unable to detach from the outcome.

Suggested Activities:

1. Keeping the above in mind, try to spend today focused on what's wonderful for you (knowing that what's good for you is good for him).

2. If you find that the alcoholic asks to go to treatment, and if you can help, make sure you spend the rest of that day doing a *fun* thing for you—so that the outcome is *less important* to you.

25
Vacillation Is Okay:
You're Not Crazy

Accept the things you cannot change.
Develop courage to change the things you can.
Pray for wisdom to know the difference.
And acknowledge that your fears may tell you that
it's virtuous to stay in and accept a situation.

Sometimes the easiest way to handle a mountain is just to go around it rather than to climb over it. If you find yourself facing really difficult problems and situations that you think you should handle but know you can't, sometimes it's better just to leave that problem alone. Say to yourself that it's an area of your life that you just can't manage at the moment, surrender it to your Higher Power and go about the business of the rest of your life.

Therapists who deal with regressed schizophrenics in the back wards of mental hospitals are often taught not to deal with them in the area of their very severe mental problems, but to spend the therapy sessions instead bolstering them up in areas in which they have previously done well. This would involve talking about areas in which they were able to function before and in which they were able to work—about ball games, about sewing, about all kinds of pleasant, non-emotionally-laden subjects. After several visits with these people, therapists get their attention. They stop focusing on their problems, which are, for the moment, insurmountable, and they start gaining self-esteem in some areas of their lives.

What follows is that the therapists build up the patients' self-esteem. They help them to add positive parts to their lives. Finally, in looking at the totality, the patient sees that his problem is smaller—more in perspective. They see that they have more positive things than negative things in their lives. Then the therapist can start whittling away at the negative.

When you're in the middle of a severe problem with an alcoholic, you can feel simultaneously crazy, despairing and furious. That's not necessarily the time to take the problem and deal with it. It *is* the time to focus in on areas of your life where you have strength, where you function well and concentrate on building those areas up.

The first step is getting a perspective on the problem. *Then* you can begin to deal with guilt, and fear.

One of the ways to drop the guilt is to realize that

when you feel guilty, that is your disease talking. His disease tells him that he has all kinds of reasons to drink and that he doesn't have a drinking problem. That's how his disease gets him to continue drinking. Your disease tells you that you have something to feel guilty about. That's how it keeps you in situations that make you feel crazy and angry.

If you can tell yourself over and over again that you know the source of your guilt feelings—that "It's your disease talking"—then it's easier to remember that the healthy thing to do is to let go of the guilt. Let his problem *be* his problem; only when he realizes that it *is* his problem will *he* want to do something about it.

Once you've settled down and things are in perspective and you've taken a deep breath and said, "Okay, I'm not dealing out of desperation. But what can I do to get off of this treadmill? I'm sick and tired of all the fights, of him leaving and me begging him to come back and then getting angry when he *does* come back, and so on. What can I do?"

One of the things you can do is to say to yourself, "All right, I'm going to make some kind of temporary decision right now. No, I'm not even going to make it a big deal and call it a decision. I'm going to call it a temporary choice. And I'm going to live with this choice for the time being in order to get some relief from it all. I need some peace, because my family situation is in bad shape, and my family and myself are being thoroughly traumatized by it all. My choice may not be the best answer, but I think that it is the lesser of the two evils for right now. Even if it's a mistake, that's all it is. *God's not going to punish me for making mistakes.* He expects me to be human, not infallible. Also, if I stay with one choice for right now, for however long that might be, then I can get enough evenness in my life to be able to think calmly about what to do in the long run. Maybe right now is not the time to make a long-range choice. Whatever I choose for right now, I can see it as a temporary measure, one that is not irretrievable."

Then you can double up on Al-Anon meetings, and/or go to counseling, or whatever you have to do it get some peace back into your life. This will give you a basis from which you can make long-term choices about what's best for you. It's also very important to acknowledge to yourself that this vacillation is not a further indication that you are crazy. You are reacting to a very difficult situation like a normal human being. The fact is that if you were accidentally locked up in a mental hospital with no way to get out for as long as you've been locked up with your alcoholic, I think you would be reacting as crazily as you are now. It would be almost inevitable. As Al-Anon says in its introduction to each meeting, "Living with an alcoholic is too much for most of us." That's the truth.

"Stronger by weakness, wiser, men become." (Edmund Waller)

Write On:

1. If you're in the middle of a back-and-forth situation with your alcoholic spouse, stop and list some of the options that would give you a much-needed, peaceful break. Ideas: a cheap or free vacation at a relative's house; a weekend at a health spa.

2. Try to follow through and give yourself this break. Sometimes not trying to solve a problem is, at that time, the problem's solution.

Suggested Activity:

Tell yourself daily that God does not view your situation in a you-made-your-bed-now-lie-in-it fashion. Life is too short for that. You have the right to find happiness—the right to find freedom from a situation that makes you unhappy.

26

If You're Remarried to Your Second Alcoholic, or You've Remarried the Same One or You're Dating a Man with a Drinking Problem

If you go for help, you will know:
You are getting stronger.
You are gaining in self-esteem.
You are learning to trust God and yourself.

I feel that one of the pitfalls to watch out for is what Maryann was telling me about when she came into counseling. She was the child of two alcoholics and, during her early twenties, she found herself in a number of destructive relationships with drinking alcoholics, or alcoholics who kept having slips in and out of AA. Then she found herself in a very good relationship. She described this man to me as being perfect. She told me how wonderful he was. And a "red light" went on in my mind. Why? Because she used to talk like that about her first husband. When she first met him she thought he was all wonderful and terrific; then they got married and the trouble began.

Now she was out on her own. She had finally gotten herself together and was supporting herself and her child. But now she had found another man with whom she was repeating the same pattern. She thought he was terrific; everybody liked him, and he wasn't an alcoholic. But there was a problem; she couldn't seem to get him to be close to her.

She dropped out of counseling for a while, and then I heard from her a few months later. She came in feeling rather distraught because she found out that this terrific man had been staying with his ex-wife when he wasn't around her. I talked to her about the way children of alcoholics, people who *were* married to alcoholics or people who have lived for a long time in an alcoholic situation, sometimes get out of one bad situation and then get involved with someone who is not quite as destructive and who, by comparison, looks good. I told her that what I felt was at the bottom of behavior of this type was a lack of self-trust, a lack of trust in one's own instincts to tell you when something is good or not. There is also often a lack of trust in oneself, a belief that one lacks the staying power necessary to wait, to endure lonely times between relationships, to say no to a relationship that one knows will turn out badly. There can also be a lack of trust in one's own ability to get through the time that is necessary to get that self-esteem. Most members of alcoholic families don't know that they have the capacity to get that self-esteem and attract someone who has an equal amount of self-esteem. Self-esteem attracts the same amount of self-esteem, so you usually have to get healthy before you can attract someone healthy. *What is lacking in that family is not the ability, but the ability to trust themselves that they have that ability.* They are so beaten down that they don't believe they possess any intrinsically worthwhile qualities. They don't have trust in themselves, in their own strength. It's the mirror opposite of the alcoholic; the drinking alcoholic claims that he has all the strength and that he's totally independent—but he doesn't and he's not. And the family members think they don't have any strength and that they're totally dependent, while actually they have lots of strength and they are a lot more independent than they believe themselves to be. They just have to be shown that this is in fact the case.

Another blind spot families of alcoholics often have is best exemplified by Carey's story. Her husband of forty-two years passed away. He had been a drinking alcoholic and a vicious one; at one point he had left her and gone to live with another woman. Even after that she had taken him back, but things still had gotten worse and worse. He deteriorated mentally, physically and spiritually. He lost his job and spent all of his retirement benefits until there was nothing left. She found it necessary, at a very late stage of life, to go out and work at two jobs in order to pay the hospital bills. In spite of the fact that she was doing her best to care for him, he remained mean and cruel.

After his death, she found herself mourning not just him, but her investment in all those years of insanity. Not wanting to waste her time looking back, however, she tried to quickly gather herself together and start her new life. This in itself was very commendable, considering all that she had been through. She started going out with friends, playing bridge again and going on trips. She seemed to be doing quite well. But there was something missing. Of course she missed the companionship of a man. But she was missing something else too. Unknown to herself, what Carey was missing was the excited misery that is always part of a relationship with a drinking alcoholic. She didn't know how to seek excitement in healthy channels; she didn't have the behavior patterns necessary. She didn't really talk to anybody about how to find healthy relationships. So she went blindly looking for the excited misery again.

She went to a festival that was being held by members of her ethnic group. A certain small group that was known to be rowdy was present at the gathering. Generally, one could see that there was probably a lot of alcoholism involved, but on the surface it seemed like a party—fun. She got caught up with a man in that group who was a widower and who was obviously an alcoholic. But he was not flat on his back (unlike her husband during the last decade of their marriage) and he was not vicious. He did not flirt with every other woman in sight. *She* was the woman he flirted with. He was sparkling and lively and fun and totally charming—and alcoholic. He swept her off her feet and she felt for the first time in nearly fifty years like she was in love again. No amount of talking was going to prevent her from going headlong into that relationship.

It wasn't until several months later, by which time she was pretty deeply involved, that he dropped his facade of the fun guy and started acting out all the rotten junk of drinking alcoholic behavior. She started slipping back into the typical patterns of dealing with that, which included screaming, yelling, feeling bad and saying, "My God, how did I get myself into this again?"

Karen found herself in a similar kind of situation. She had married a man who was an alcoholic and had divorced him several years later. After she had gotten herself together again, when the scars had healed and she had nearly forgotten all his alcoholic junk, he called her up. He knew what strings to pluck. He brought her some expensive gifts, was very charming and acted as if he was going to be doing the giving this time instead of the taking. She felt that he had changed, even though he was still drinking. They got back together again and remarried. Three days after the wedding he took off his mask. He stopped hiding and controlling his drinking and it all started all over again. Four months later, Karen was in a suicidal depression.

I think that we all have a tendency to *forget the facts.* We don't want to remember them. They seem too horrible; in fact, they seem *so* bizarre and *so* horrible (which, by the way, they are) that we tend to think to ourselves that we must really be exaggerating. We find it impossible to believe that things really were that bad.

It's a good idea to *remember the facts.* It might even be a good idea to keep a diary of the facts—of how actually horrible things *were,* so that, if you ever have any future doubts, if you ever want to ask yourself, "Was it really all that terrible?" you'll be able to look in your diary and know that it really was.

It's good when you're writing this diary to avoid putting much emotion in it, so you won't look back and say, "It couldn't have been that bad. I was just hysterical at the time," and therefore discount what the diary has to say. Just try to stick to the facts as if you were a dispassionate, disinterested, clinical third party, looking on, making observations, doing reporting. If you write the diary in that manner you will find that, if you ever need to look back in it, it will be a good reminder of what the facts really were.

However, it's not good to look back on that diary when there's no logical, rational reason to look into it. Don't dredge up the old junk. Let sleeping dogs lie.

Are you trying to get into some excited misery? Are you bored? If you're bored, reading a diary is no way to fill in the gap. You're just going to make yourself feel bad, so why look at it? It is only to be looked at for educational purposes, when you find yourself drawn to old junk that you really want to escape from.

Another way to help extricate yourself from a bad situation is not to beat on yourself. It's really important to say, "Okay, I made a mistake. I'm not God; I'm just a person. Therefore, I can be *expected* to make mistakes. That's what a person does. In fact, making mistakes can be very important because they teach us something. What I have to do now is find the best way to extricate myself from the consequences of this mistake and go on from there."

Now, once you've extricated yourself from the situation, what is the best way *not* to make the same mistake again? Let yourself acknowledge at this point in your life the depth of your need to get into unhealthy situations. Realize, as you keep getting well, that this need is going to diminish tremendously.

But what do you do right now about that need? Well, you tell yourself the truth. If you don't tell yourself the truth, you will tend to minimize what the situation actually *is*. And if you minimize in this way, then you won't be able to get well. Tell yourself that you are addicted to sick situations and sick people. That's what's really going on.

How do people extricate themselves from sick, self-destructive stuff when they are addicted to a certain kind of thing? Well, what do people do in Alcoholics Anonymous? They go to their meetings one day at a time. They ask God one day at a time to keep them out of destructive, alcoholic situations; they grit their teeth when they want to drink and the physical compulsion comes over them; they do anything to not take that drink. They postpone it an hour or a day; they sit in a bathtub for three hours so they don't go to the bar; they go for long walks (leaving all of their money at home). They call somebody on the phone and stay on the phone all night if they have to. They do anything to postpone that urge. Because the urge *does* pass. It doesn't stick around twenty-four hours a day. They put other thoughts in their minds because they realize that two thoughts can't occupy the same mind at one time.

Thus, it might be a good idea to go to open AA meetings and listen to stories of how people got over their addiction one day at a time. This helps to get away from thinking in terms of months or years and coming to learn that one day at a time is best and that you should be proud of yourself and very grateful to God that He gave you the strength to do it that way. You should also have tremendous hope and realize that every day you put off going into a sick situation, you're getting stronger, tremendously stronger in ways that you don't even realize. It's beneath the surface, for the most part. You're getting self-esteem. You're gaining a sense of self in the best sense, in the sense of realizing your strength and depending on God's strength, instead of depending on a sick person. And you're moving slowly but surely towards the point where you will only be drawn towards people who feel good about themselves, too, and who can love in a total way.

"As soon as you trust yourself, you will know how to live." (Johann Wolfgang Von Goethe)

Write On:

If you are dating someone who is not good for you, but you feel driven and can't stop, tell yourself instead that you choose not to stop. This will help you feel more capable of stopping yourself in the future. Try to determine what *need* he is truly fulfilling. Don't worry about self-image; self-honesty can save you years of pain.

Suggested Activity:

Can meeting that need be postponed, one day at a time? Can you try for one hour? Even if you manage to succeed for only one hour, you'll know that you can do it again.

197

Guide for Help

If you would like information about meeting schedules, literature and other services of Alcoholics Anonymous, Al-Anon or Al-Ateen in your area, simply call Directory Assistance in your area code and ask for the number. They will be happy to have someone return your call and help you in any way they can.

The author, Toby Rice Drews, is a counselor and social worker and she is available for counseling family members. You may reach her at her home in Baltimore, MD, at (301) 243-8352.

Audiocassettes, films, newsletters, and other resources by Toby Rice Drews are available from:

Maryland Publishing
P.O. Box 19910
Baltimore, MD 21211

All of Toby's books are available
in caselots at special prices.

Any organization involved with helping
alcoholics and their families
interested in bulk order discounts can contact:

BRIDGE PUBLISHING, INC.
1-800-631-5802

Or write:
BRIDGE PUBLISHING, INC.
2500 Hamilton Blvd.
South Plainfield, NJ 07080

Educators, counselors, and health professionals
may obtain a catalog of educational aids by sending
$2.00 to:

THE HEALTH CONNECTION
Narcotics Education Incorporated
6830 Laurel Street, N.W.
Washington, D.C. 20012
USA